BREATH OF BONES™

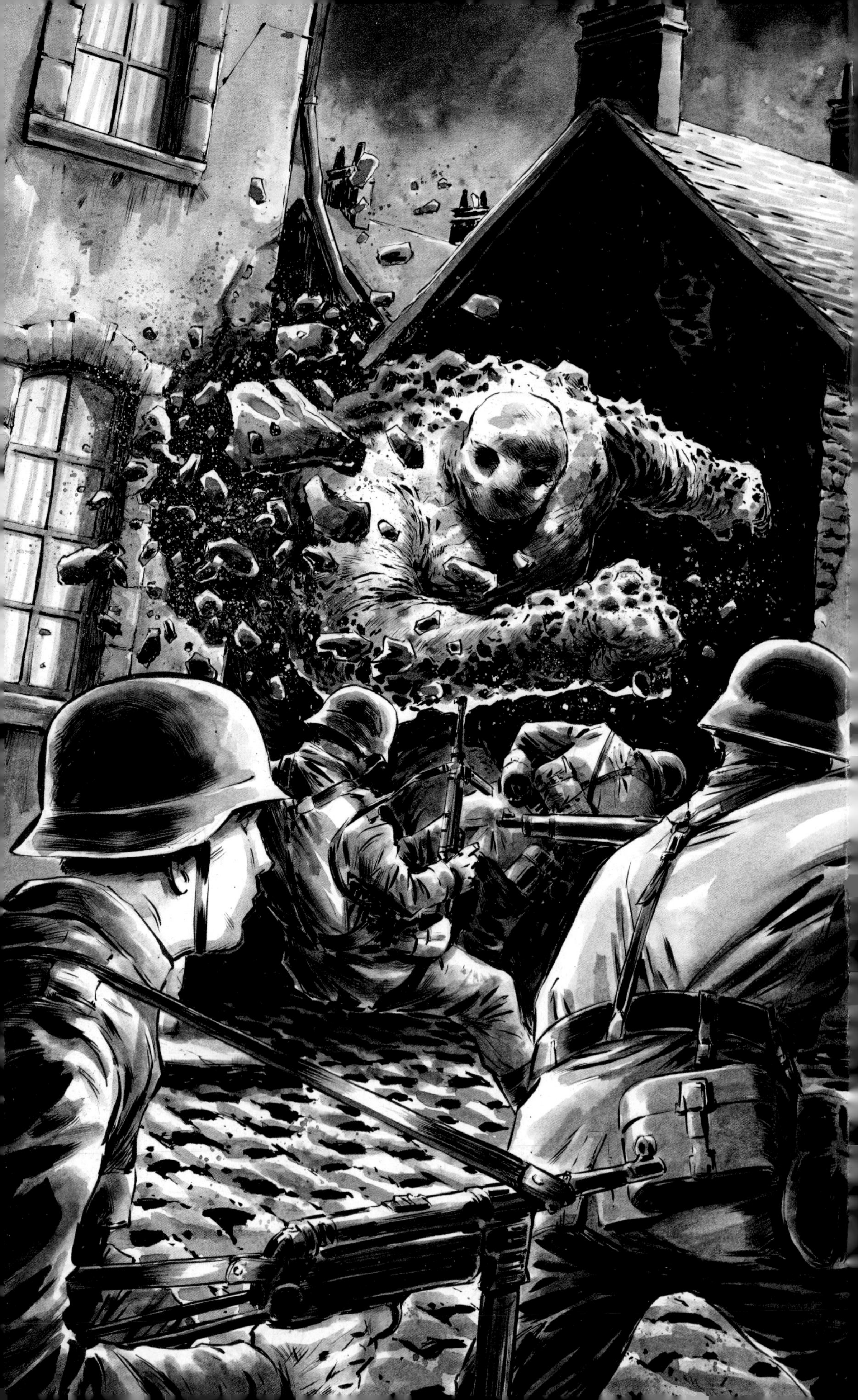

A TALE OF
THE GOLEM

Story
STEVE NILES and **MATT SANTORO**

Script
STEVE NILES

Art
DAVE WACHTER

Letters
NATE PIEKOS of BLAMBOT®

DARK HORSE BOOKS

Subjects: LCSH: World War, 1939-1945--Jews--Comic books, strips, etc. |
  Golem--Comic books, strips, etc. | Graphic novels.
Classification: LCC PN6728.B678 N55 2021 | DDC 741.5/973--dc23
LC record available at https://lccn.loc.gov/2020052321

BREATH OF BONES: A TALE OF THE GOLEM

CHAPTER ONE

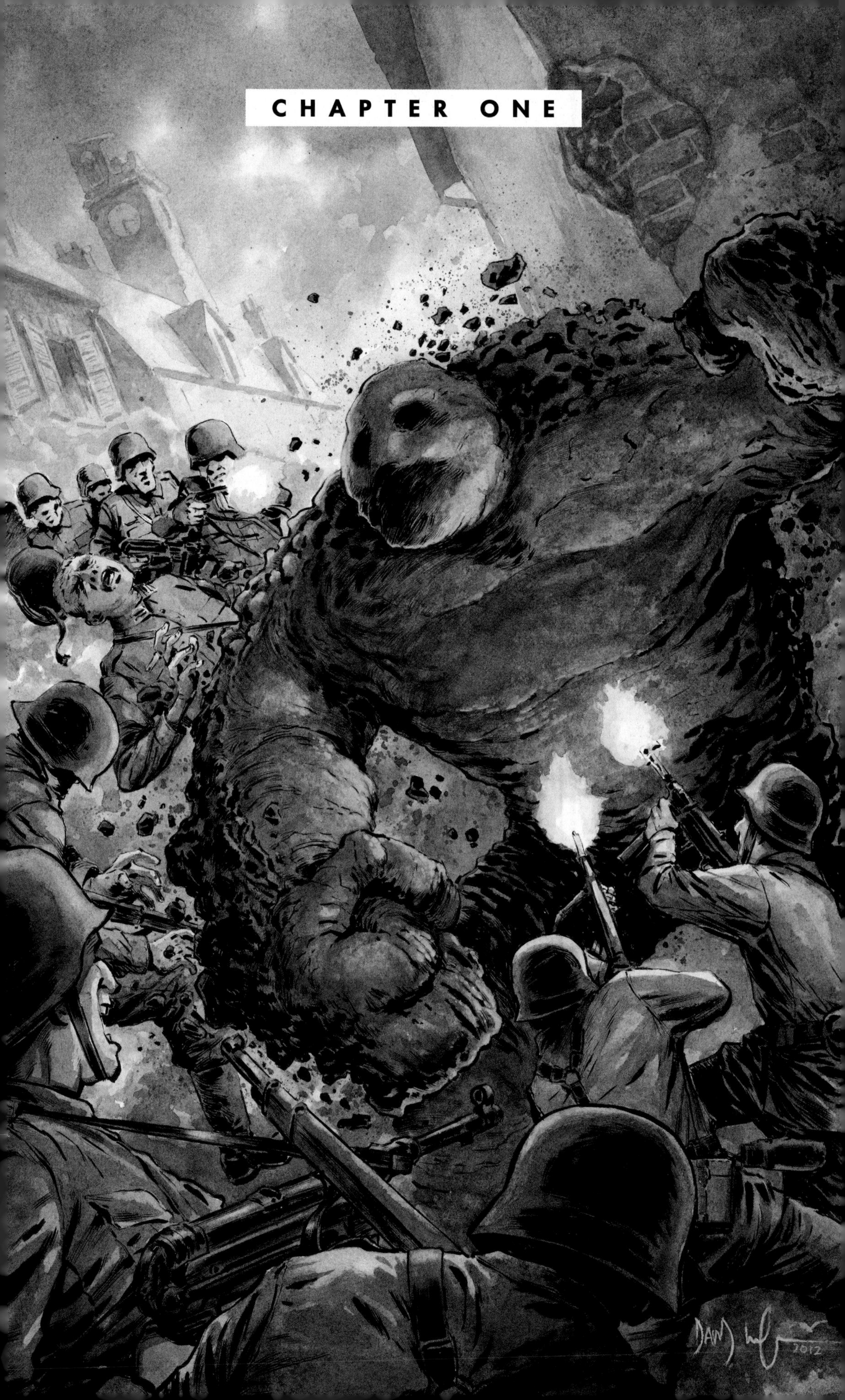

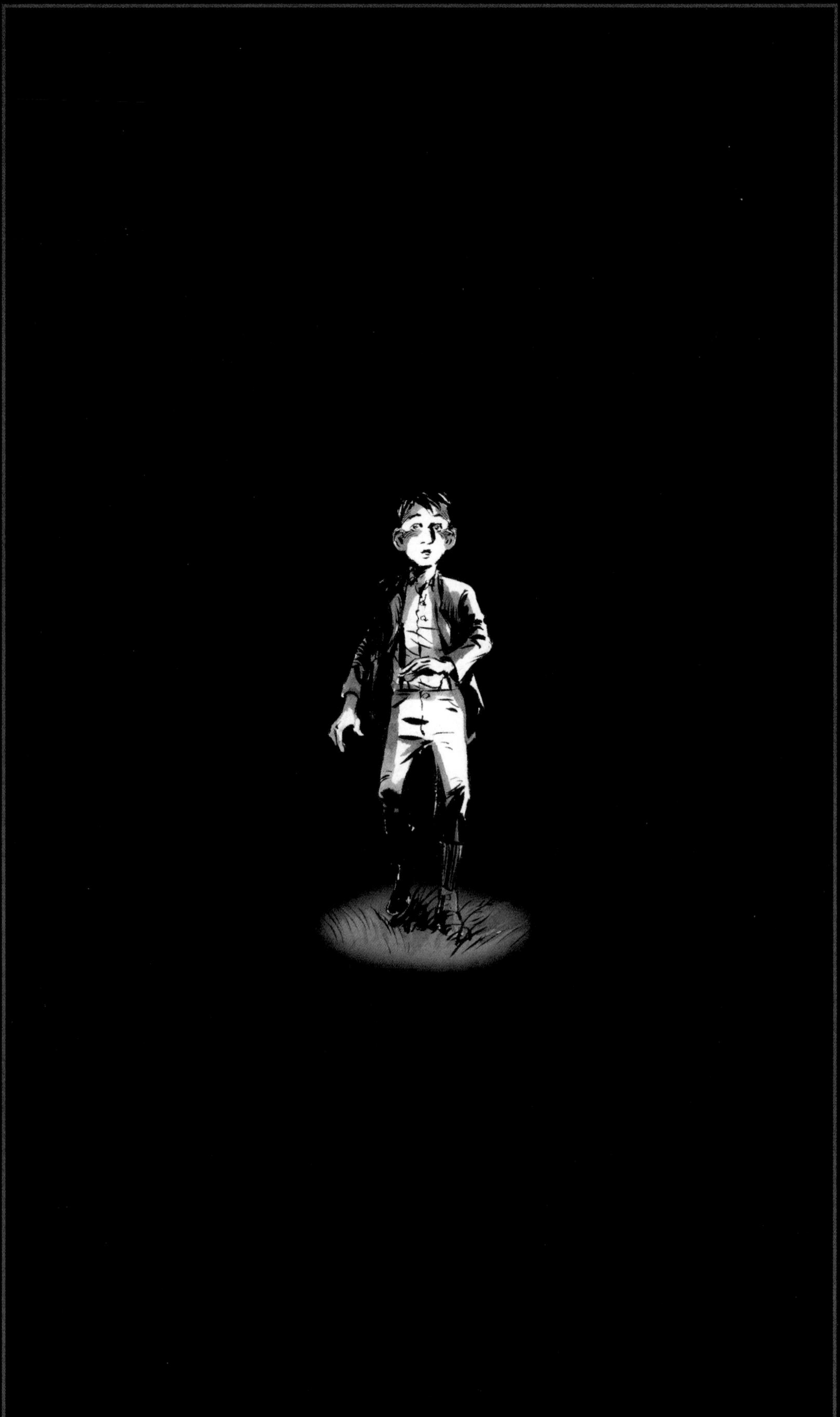

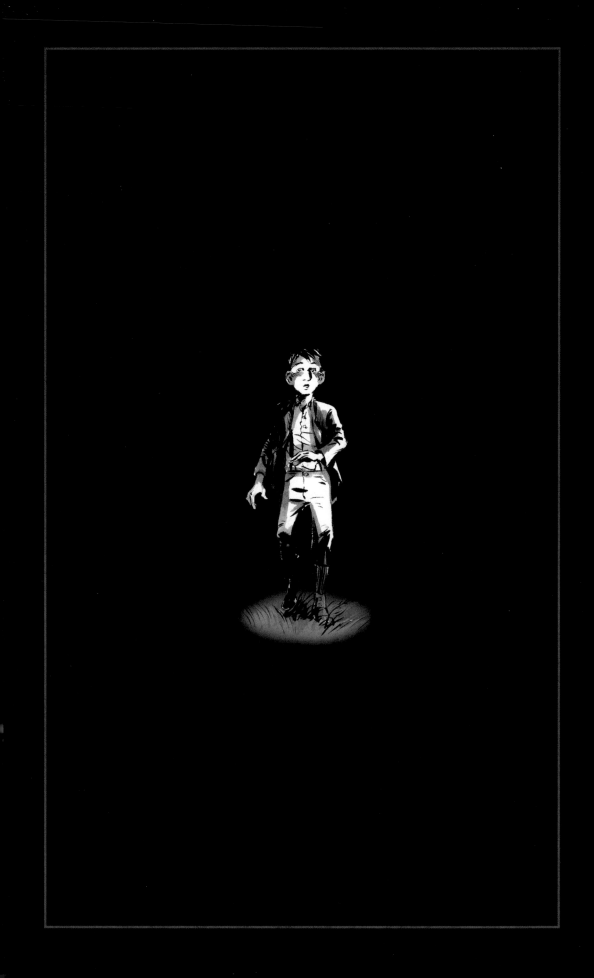

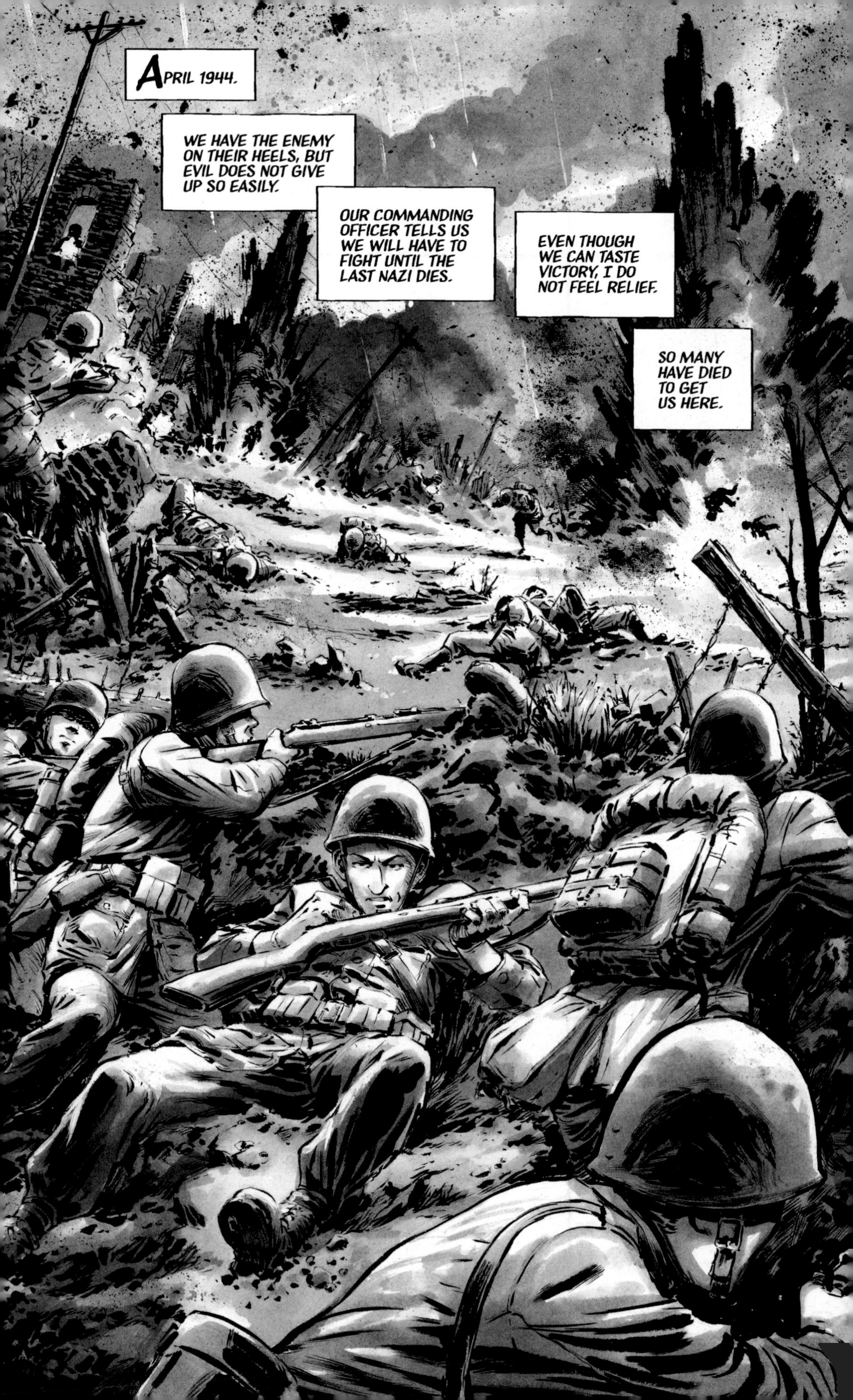
APRIL 1944.
WE HAVE THE ENEMY ON THEIR HEELS, BUT EVIL DOES NOT GIVE UP SO EASILY.
OUR COMMANDING OFFICER TELLS US WE WILL HAVE TO FIGHT UNTIL THE LAST NAZI DIES.
EVEN THOUGH WE CAN TASTE VICTORY, I DO NOT FEEL RELIEF.
SO MANY HAVE DIED TO GET US HERE.

AND ALL THOUGHTS BRING ME BACK TO MY FATHER AND MY GRANDFATHER.

I RECALL ASKING MY FATHER A SIMPLE QUESTION WHEN I WAS STILL A BOY.

"ARE THERE MONSTERS, PAPA?"

MY FATHER WAS A MAN WHO SEEMED TO ALWAYS SMILE. NO MATTER IF WORKING THE FIELDS OR STRUGGLING TO KEEP OUR FAMILY FED, HE ALWAYS MANAGED TO CURVE HIS LIPS AND SQUINT HIS EYES TO LET US KNOW EVERY- THING WOULD BE OKAY.

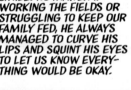

HE ONLY SHRUGGED WHEN I ASKED THIS QUESTION.

BY THE TIME I WAS FIFTEEN YEARS OF AGE, I HAD FOUND MY OWN ANSWER.

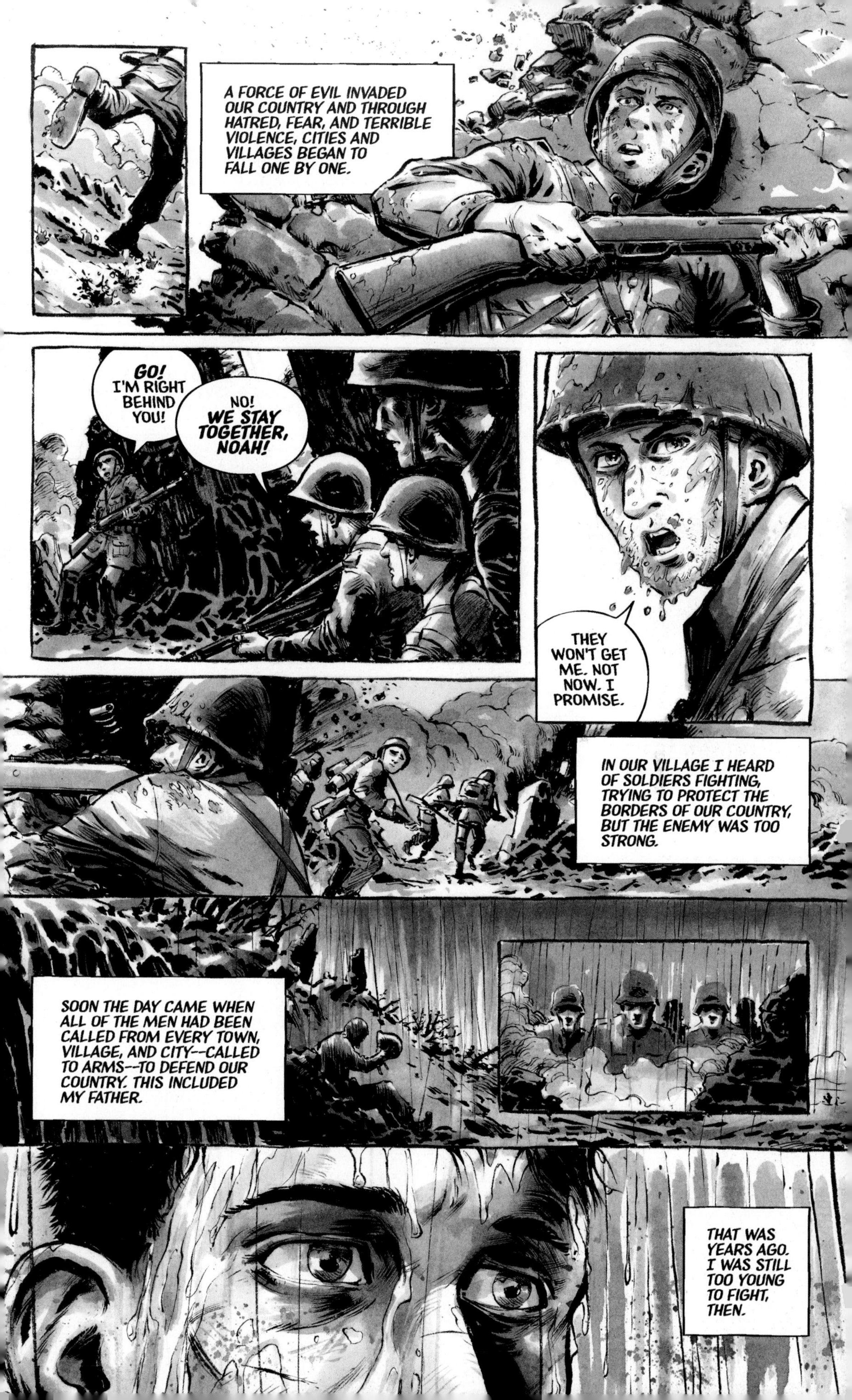
A FORCE OF EVIL INVADED OUR COUNTRY AND THROUGH HATRED, FEAR, AND TERRIBLE VIOLENCE, CITIES AND VILLAGES BEGAN TO FALL ONE BY ONE.
GO! I'M RIGHT BEHIND YOU!
NO! WE STAY TOGETHER, NOAH!
THEY WON'T GET ME. NOT NOW. I PROMISE.
IN OUR VILLAGE I HEARD OF SOLDIERS FIGHTING, TRYING TO PROTECT THE BORDERS OF OUR COUNTRY, BUT THE ENEMY WAS TOO STRONG.
SOON THE DAY CAME WHEN ALL OF THE MEN HAD BEEN CALLED FROM EVERY TOWN, VILLAGE, AND CITY--CALLED TO ARMS--TO DEFEND OUR COUNTRY. THIS INCLUDED MY FATHER.
THAT WAS YEARS AGO. I WAS STILL TOO YOUNG TO FIGHT, THEN.

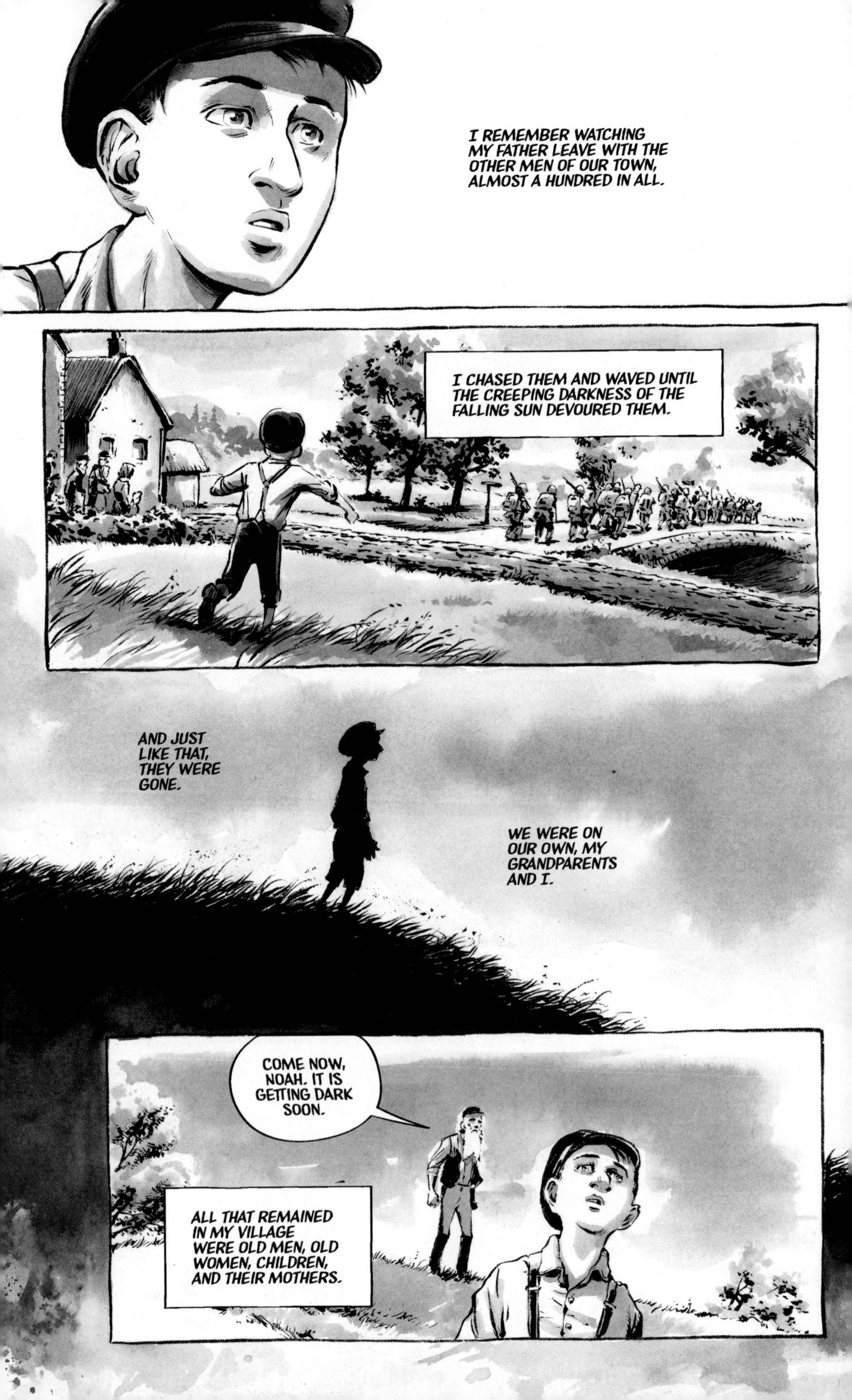
I REMEMBER WATCHING MY FATHER LEAVE WITH THE OTHER MEN OF OUR TOWN, ALMOST A HUNDRED IN ALL.
I CHASED THEM AND WAVED UNTIL THE CREEPING DARKNESS OF THE FALLING SUN DEVOURED THEM.
AND JUST LIKE THAT, THEY WERE GONE.
WE WERE ON OUR OWN, MY GRANDPARENTS AND I.
COME NOW, NOAH. IT IS GETTING DARK SOON.
ALL THAT REMAINED IN MY VILLAGE WERE OLD MEN, OLD WOMEN, CHILDREN, AND THEIR MOTHERS.

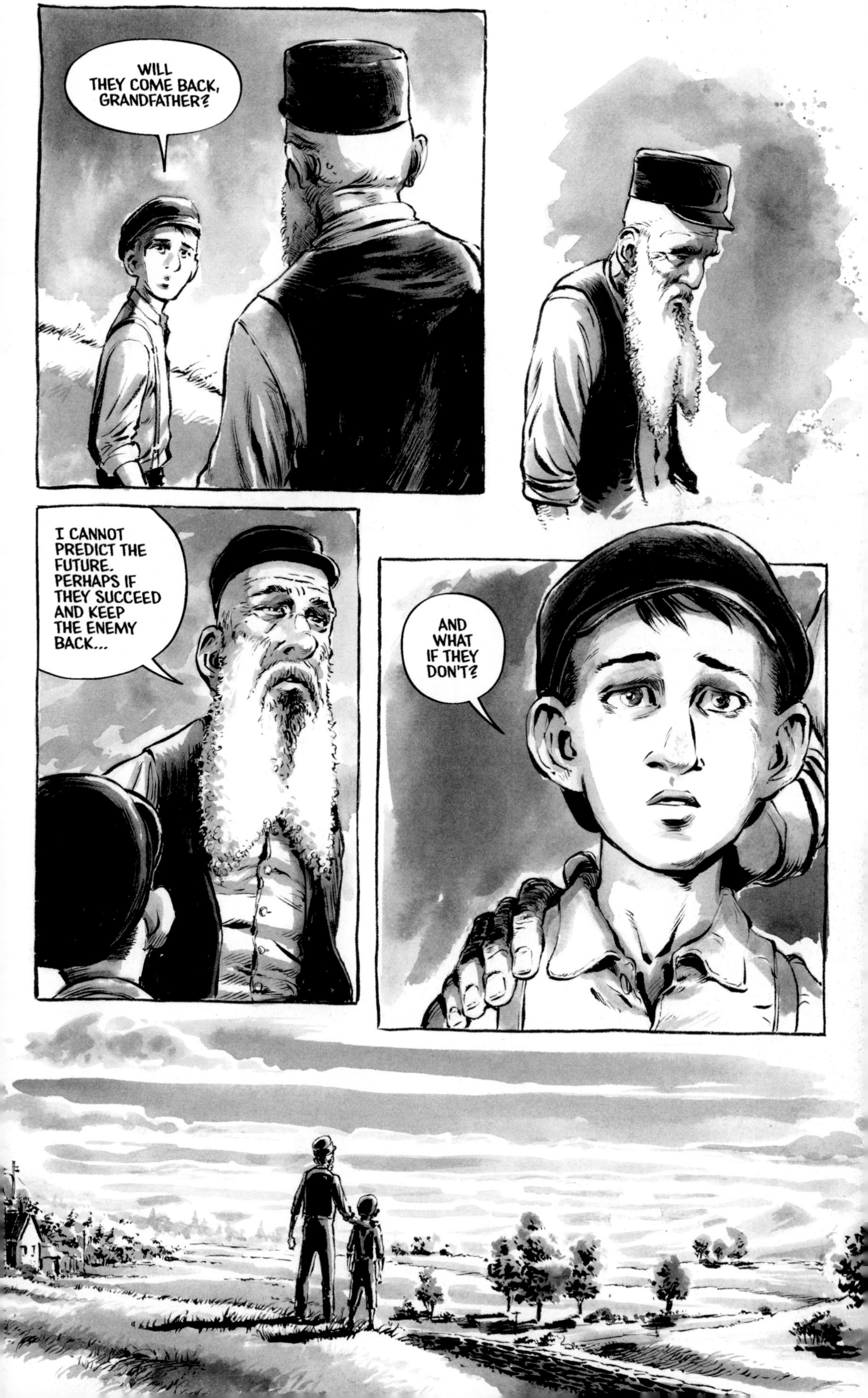
WILL THEY COME BACK, GRANDFATHER?
I CANNOT PREDICT THE FUTURE. PERHAPS IF THEY SUCCEED AND KEEP THE ENEMY BACK...
AND WHAT IF THEY DON'T?

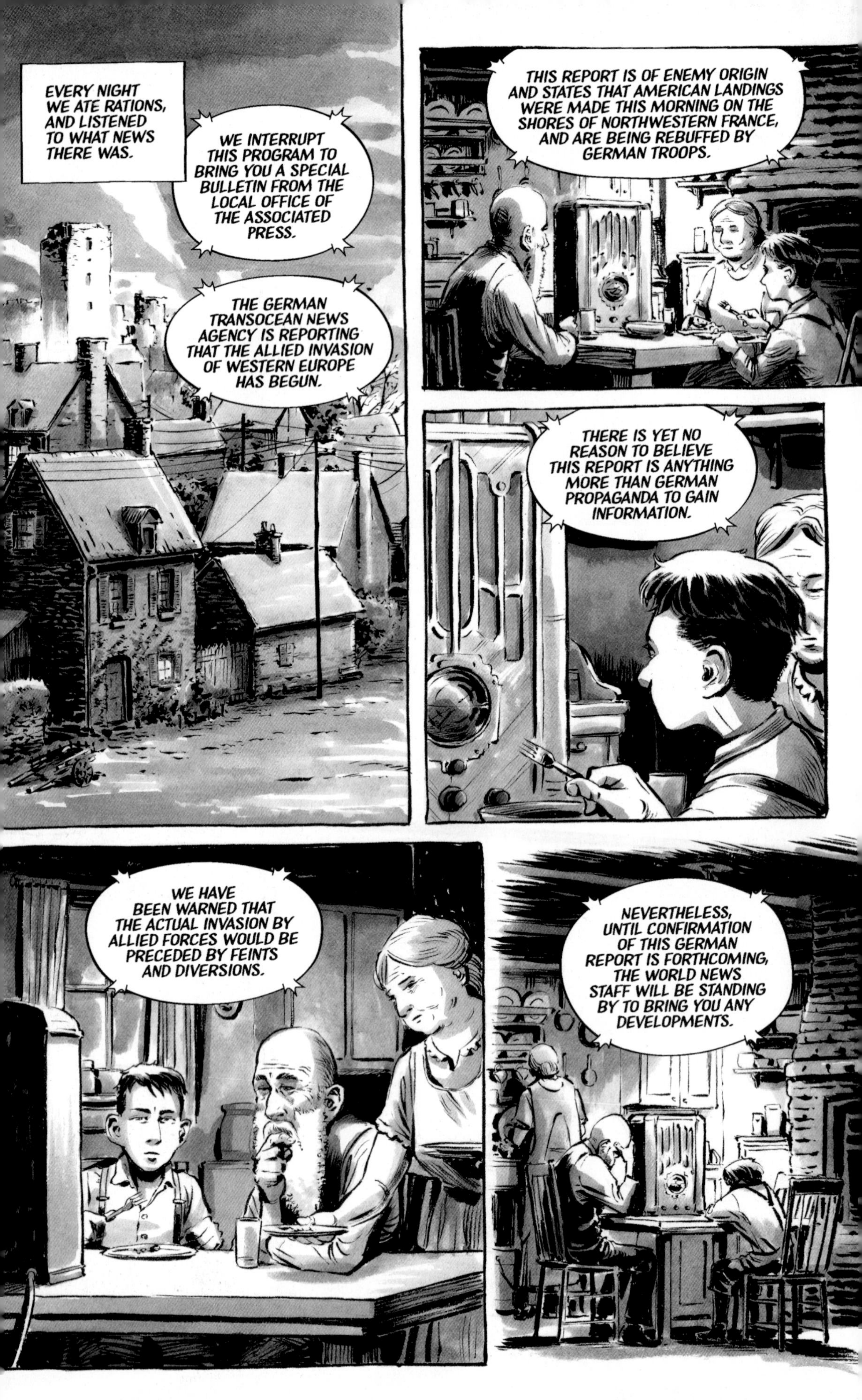
EVERY NIGHT WE ATE RATIONS, AND LISTENED TO WHAT NEWS THERE WAS.
WE INTERRUPT THIS PROGRAM TO BRING YOU A SPECIAL BULLETIN FROM THE LOCAL OFFICE OF THE ASSOCIATED PRESS.
THE GERMAN TRANSOCEAN NEWS AGENCY IS REPORTING THAT THE ALLIED INVASION OF WESTERN EUROPE HAS BEGUN.
THIS REPORT IS OF ENEMY ORIGIN AND STATES THAT AMERICAN LANDINGS WERE MADE THIS MORNING ON THE SHORES OF NORTHWESTERN FRANCE, AND ARE BEING REBUFFED BY GERMAN TROOPS.
THERE IS YET NO REASON TO BELIEVE THIS REPORT IS ANYTHING MORE THAN GERMAN PROPAGANDA TO GAIN INFORMATION.
WE HAVE BEEN WARNED THAT THE ACTUAL INVASION BY ALLIED FORCES WOULD BE PRECEDED BY FEINTS AND DIVERSIONS.
NEVERTHELESS, UNTIL CONFIRMATION OF THIS GERMAN REPORT IS FORTHCOMING, THE WORLD NEWS STAFF WILL BE STANDING BY TO BRING YOU ANY DEVELOPMENTS.

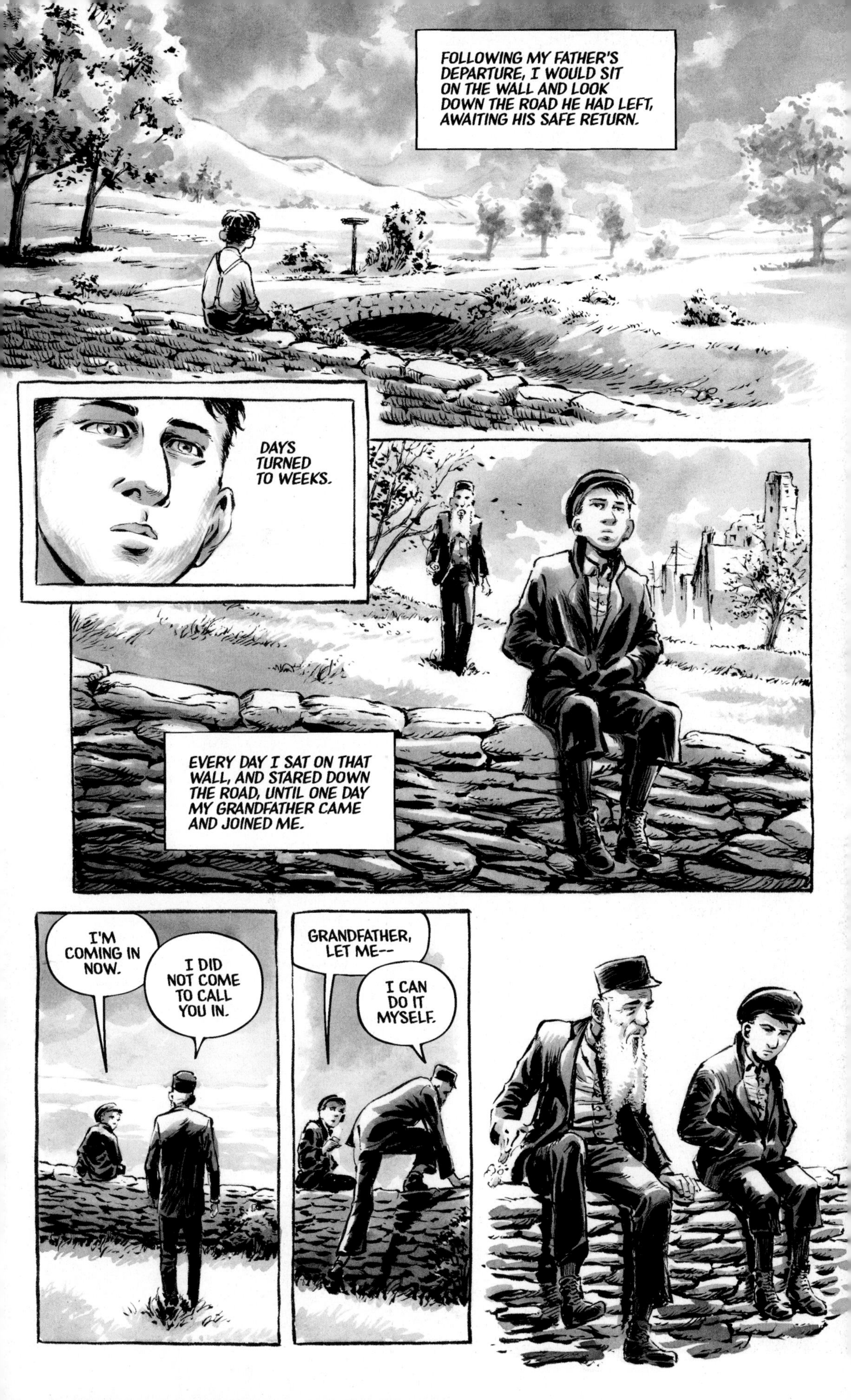
FOLLOWING MY FATHER'S DEPARTURE, I WOULD SIT ON THE WALL AND LOOK DOWN THE ROAD HE HAD LEFT, AWAITING HIS SAFE RETURN.
DAYS TURNED TO WEEKS.
EVERY DAY I SAT ON THAT WALL, AND STARED DOWN THE ROAD, UNTIL ONE DAY MY GRANDFATHER CAME AND JOINED ME.
I'M COMING IN NOW.
I DID NOT COME TO CALL YOU IN.
GRANDFATHER, LET ME--
I CAN DO IT MYSELF.

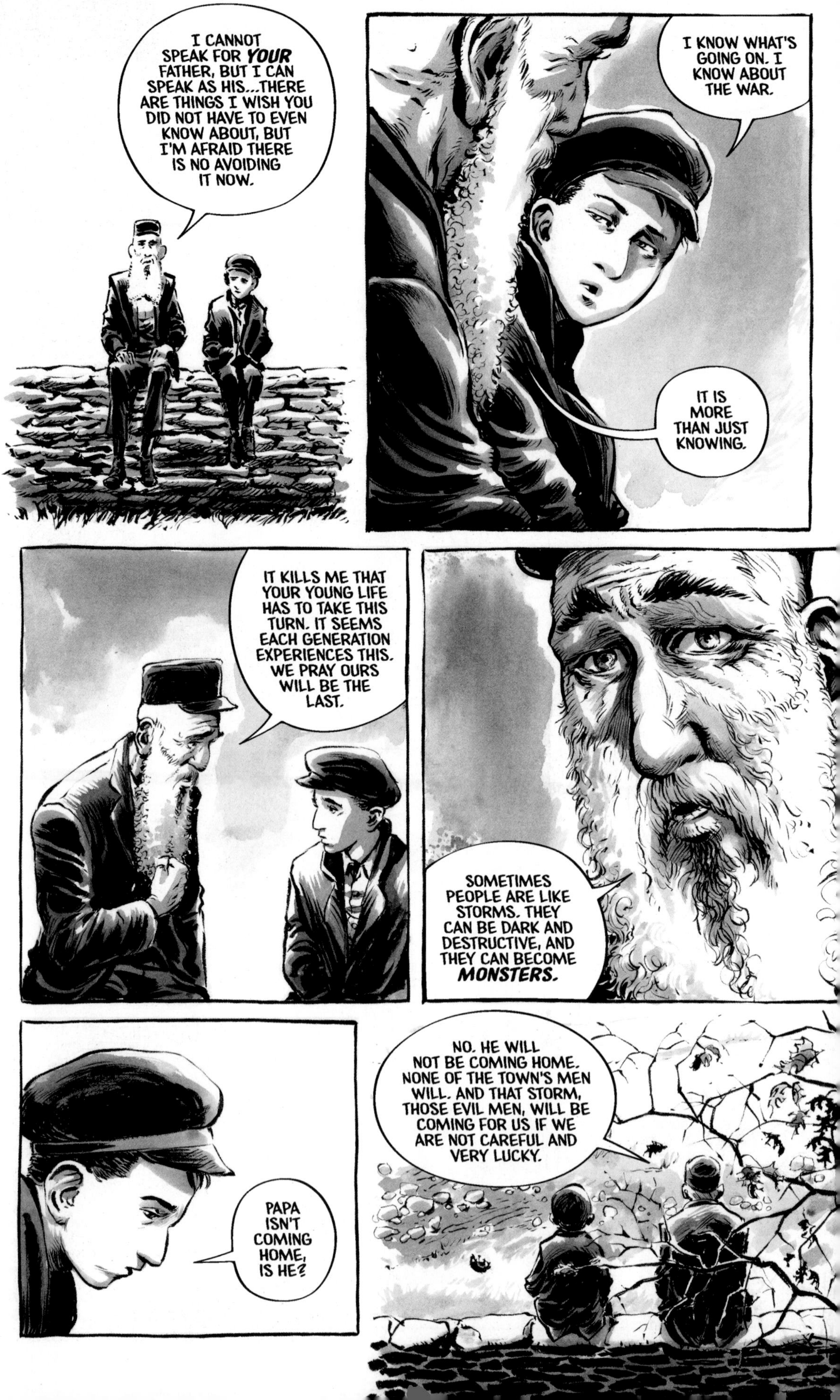
I CANNOT SPEAK FOR *YOUR* FATHER, BUT I CAN SPEAK AS HIS...THERE ARE THINGS I WISH YOU DID NOT HAVE TO EVEN KNOW ABOUT, BUT I'M AFRAID THERE IS NO AVOIDING IT NOW.
I KNOW WHAT'S GOING ON. I KNOW ABOUT THE WAR.
IT IS MORE THAN JUST KNOWING.
IT KILLS ME THAT YOUR YOUNG LIFE HAS TO TAKE THIS TURN. IT SEEMS EACH GENERATION EXPERIENCES THIS. WE PRAY OURS WILL BE THE LAST.
SOMETIMES PEOPLE ARE LIKE STORMS. THEY CAN BE DARK AND DESTRUCTIVE, AND THEY CAN BECOME ***MONSTERS.***
PAPA ISN'T COMING HOME, IS HE?
NO. HE WILL NOT BE COMING HOME. NONE OF THE TOWN'S MEN WILL. AND THAT STORM, THOSE EVIL MEN, WILL BE COMING FOR US IF WE ARE NOT CAREFUL AND VERY LUCKY.

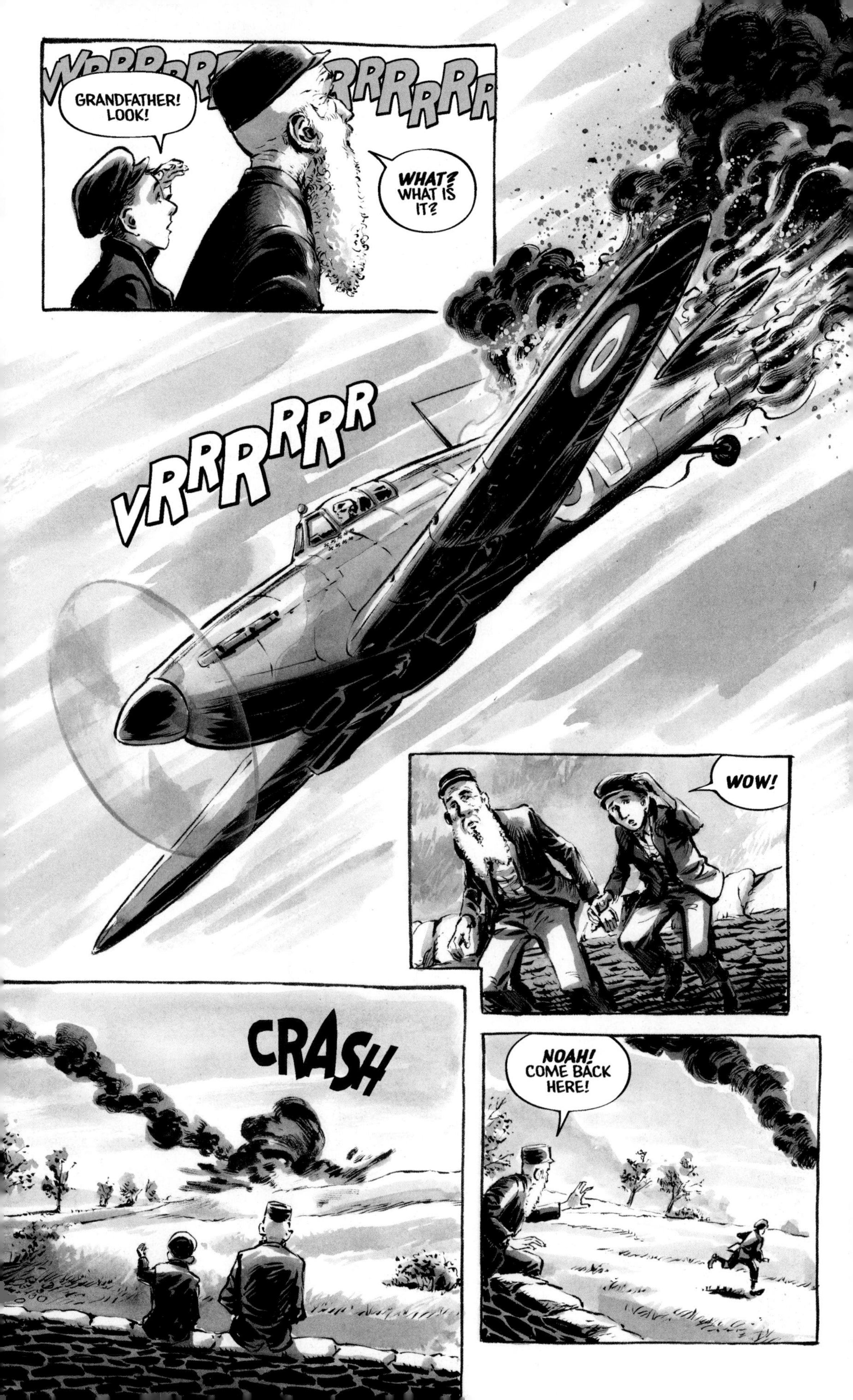
WRRRRRRRRRRRRR
GRANDFATHER! LOOK!
WHAT? WHAT IS IT?
VRRRRRR
WOW!
CRASH
NOAH! COME BACK HERE!

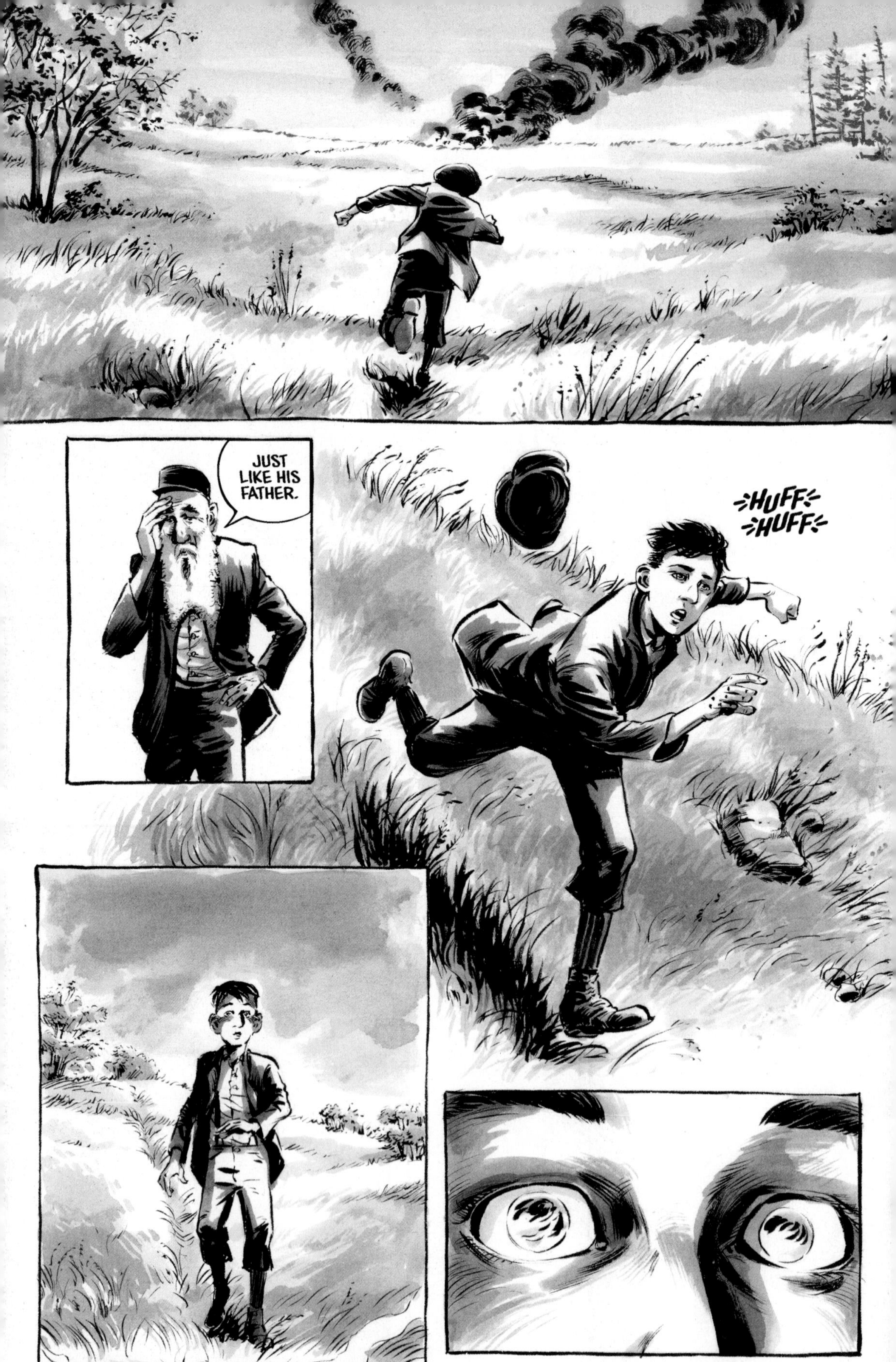
JUST LIKE HIS FATHER.
HUFF HUFF

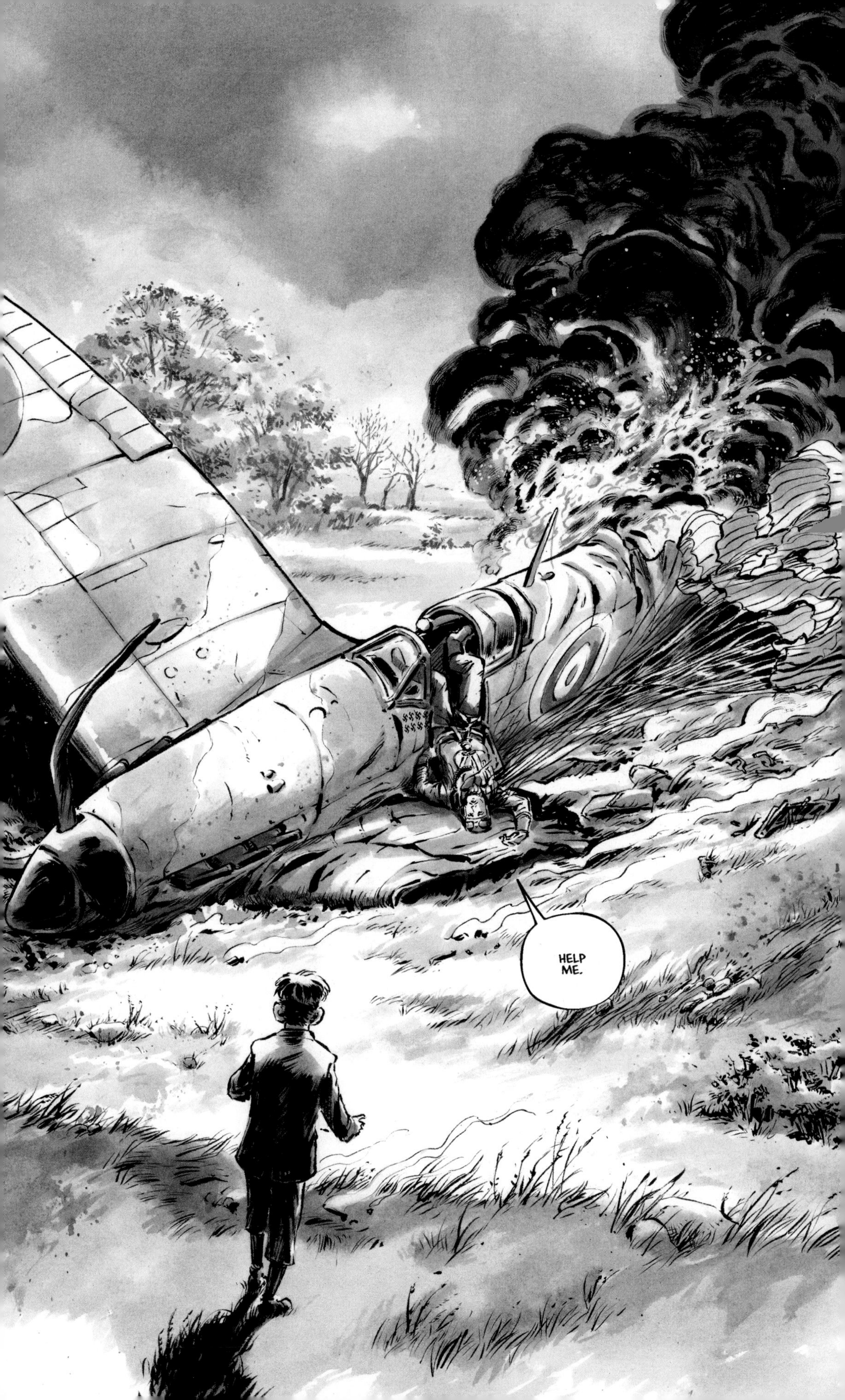
HELP ME.

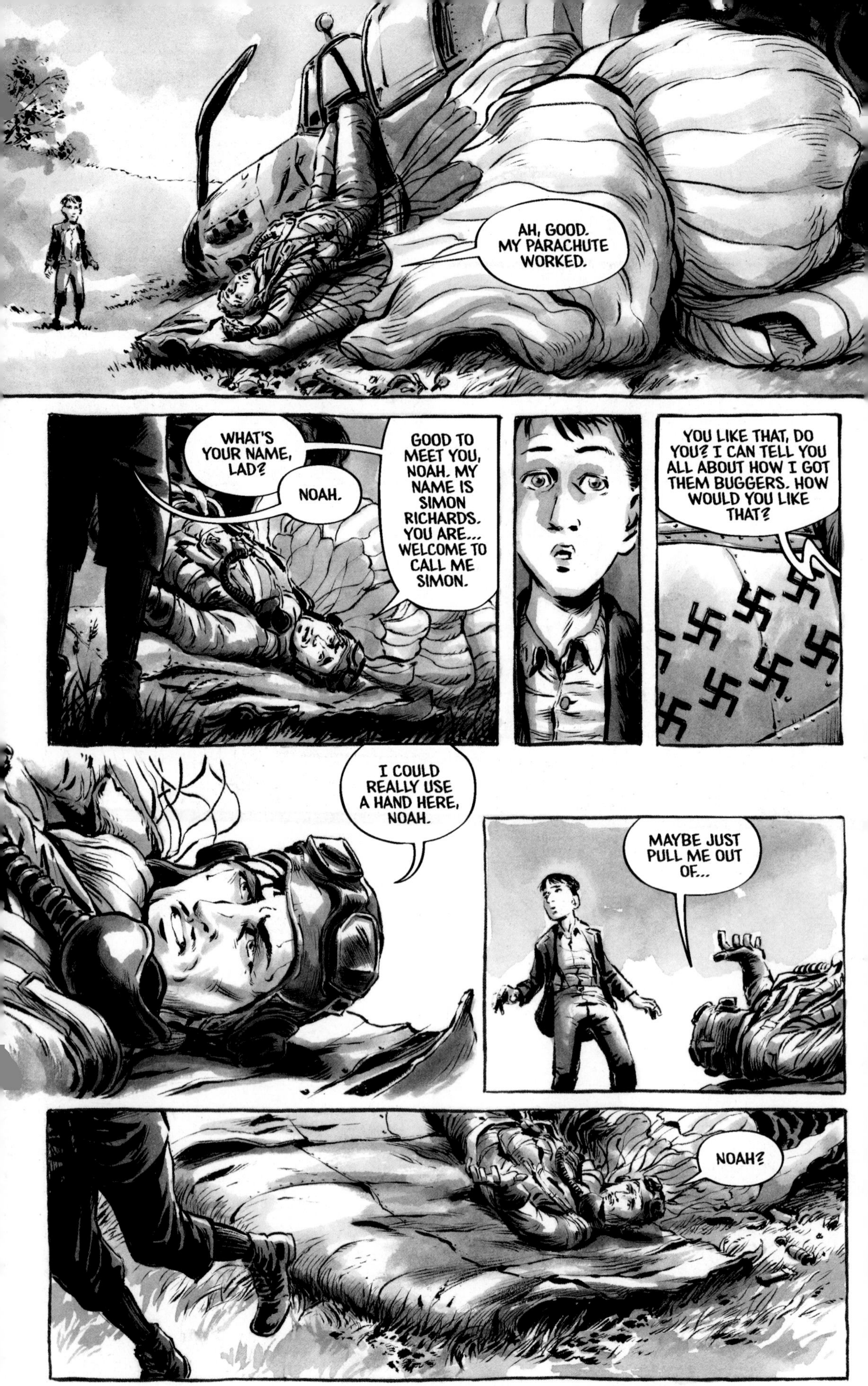
AH, GOOD. MY PARACHUTE WORKED.
WHAT'S YOUR NAME, LAD?
NOAH.
GOOD TO MEET YOU, NOAH. MY NAME IS SIMON RICHARDS. YOU ARE... WELCOME TO CALL ME SIMON.
YOU LIKE THAT, DO YOU? I CAN TELL YOU ALL ABOUT HOW I GOT THEM BUGGERS. HOW WOULD YOU LIKE THAT?
I COULD REALLY USE A HAND HERE, NOAH.
MAYBE JUST PULL ME OUT OF...
NOAH?

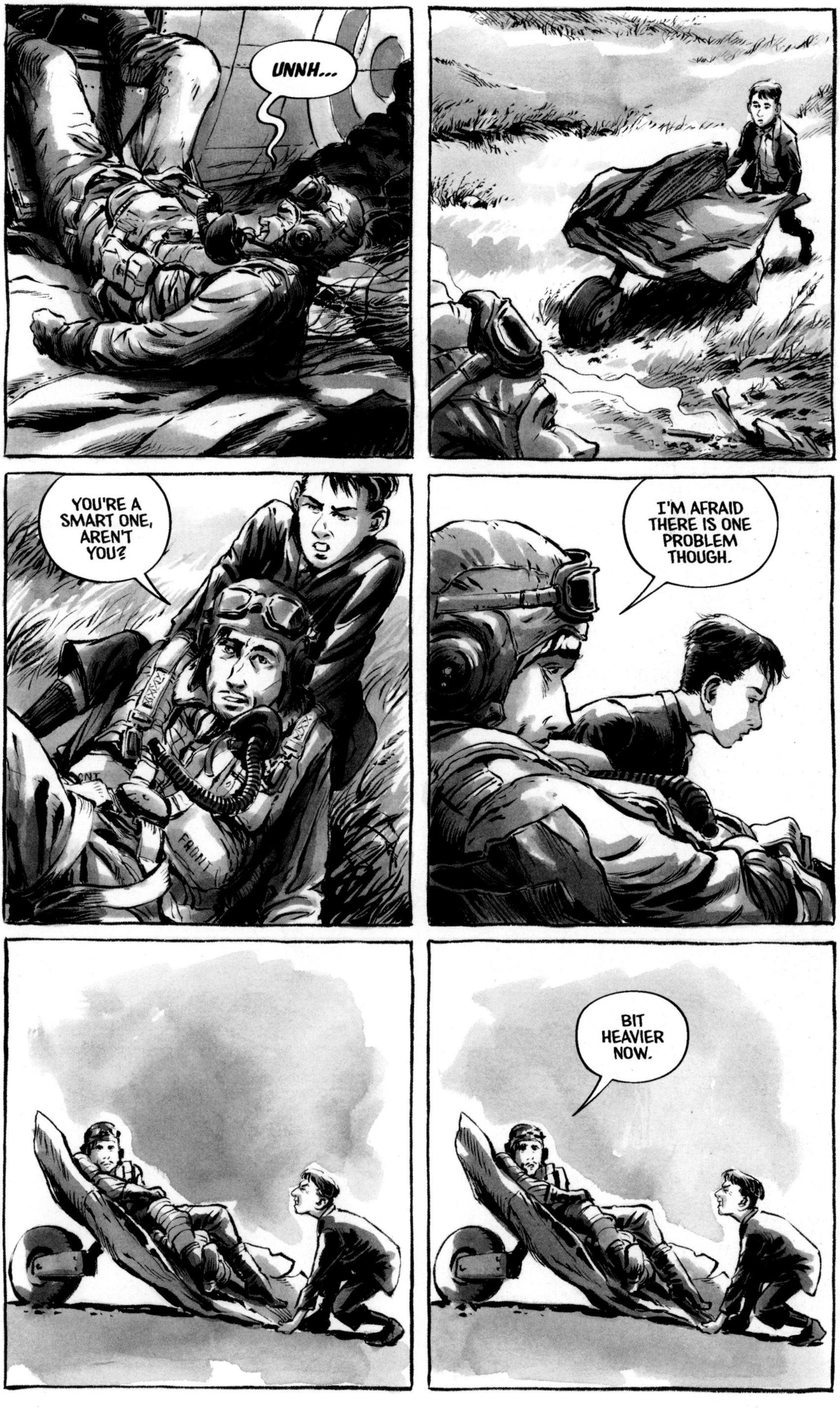
UNNH...
YOU'RE A SMART ONE, AREN'T YOU?
FRONT
FRONT
I'M AFRAID THERE IS ONE PROBLEM THOUGH.
BIT HEAVIER NOW.

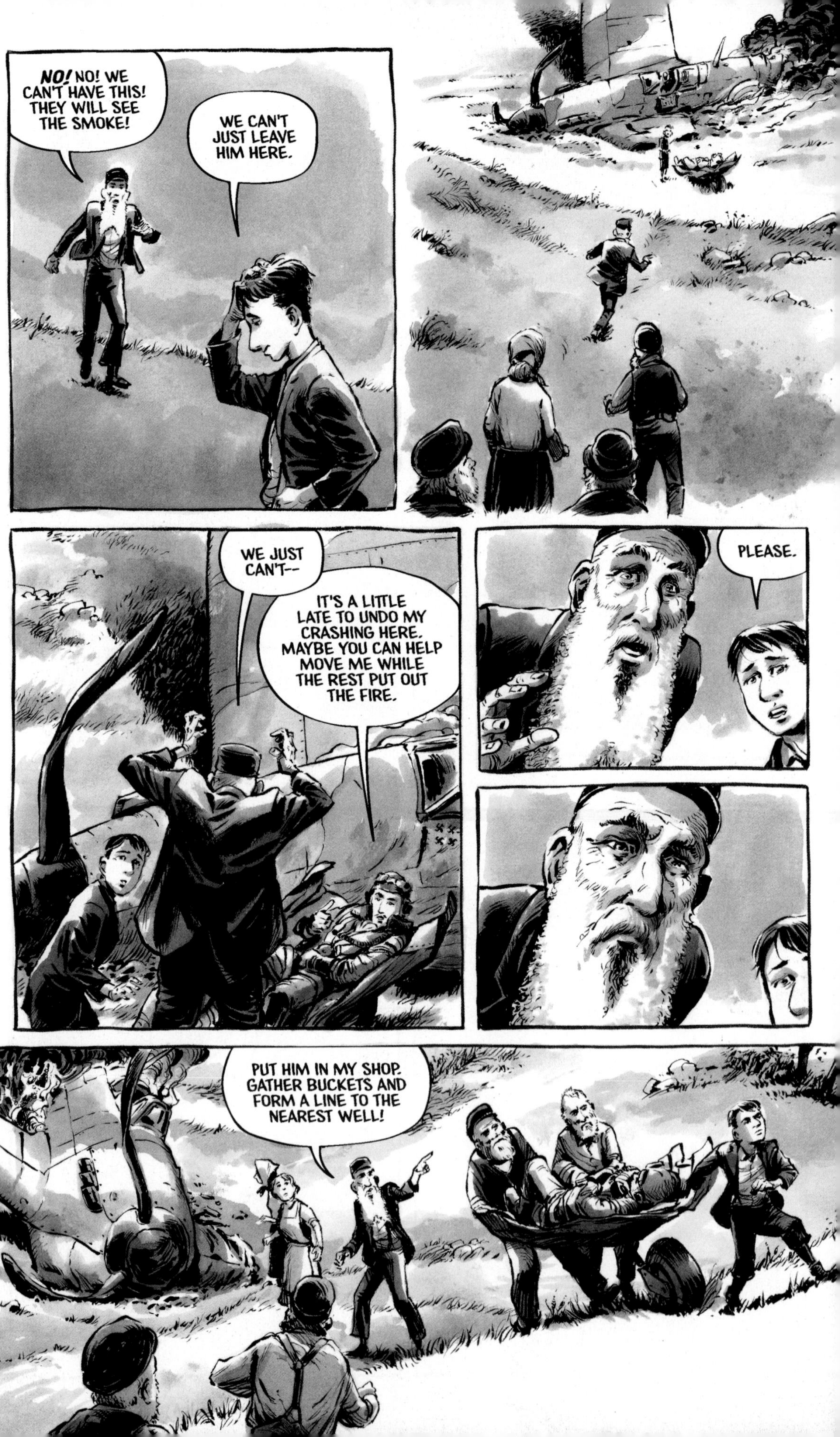
NO! NO! WE CAN'T HAVE THIS! THEY WILL SEE THE SMOKE!
WE CAN'T JUST LEAVE HIM HERE.
WE JUST CAN'T--
IT'S A LITTLE LATE TO UNDO MY CRASHING HERE. MAYBE YOU CAN HELP MOVE ME WHILE THE REST PUT OUT THE FIRE.
PLEASE.
PUT HIM IN MY SHOP. GATHER BUCKETS AND FORM A LINE TO THE NEAREST WELL!

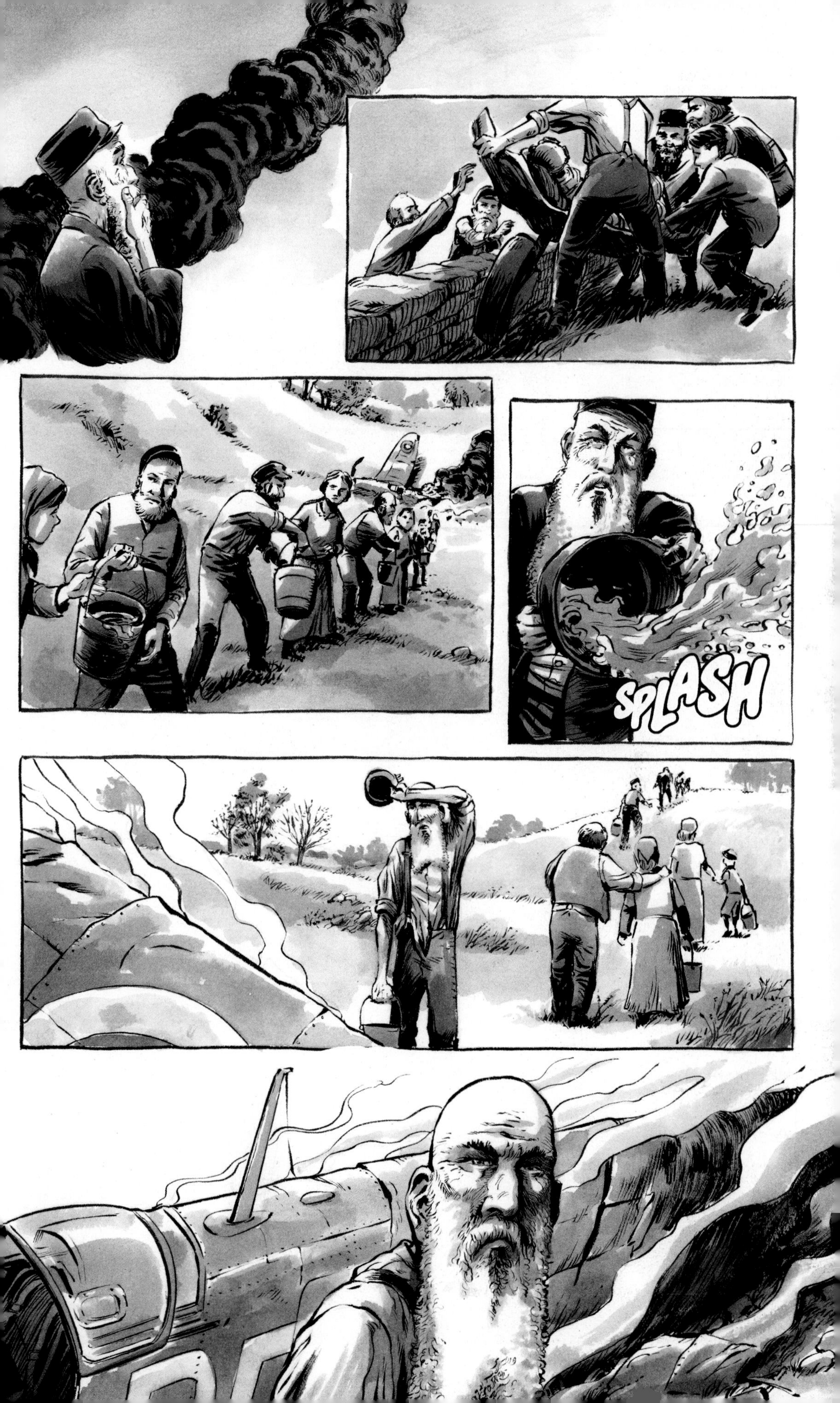
SPLASH

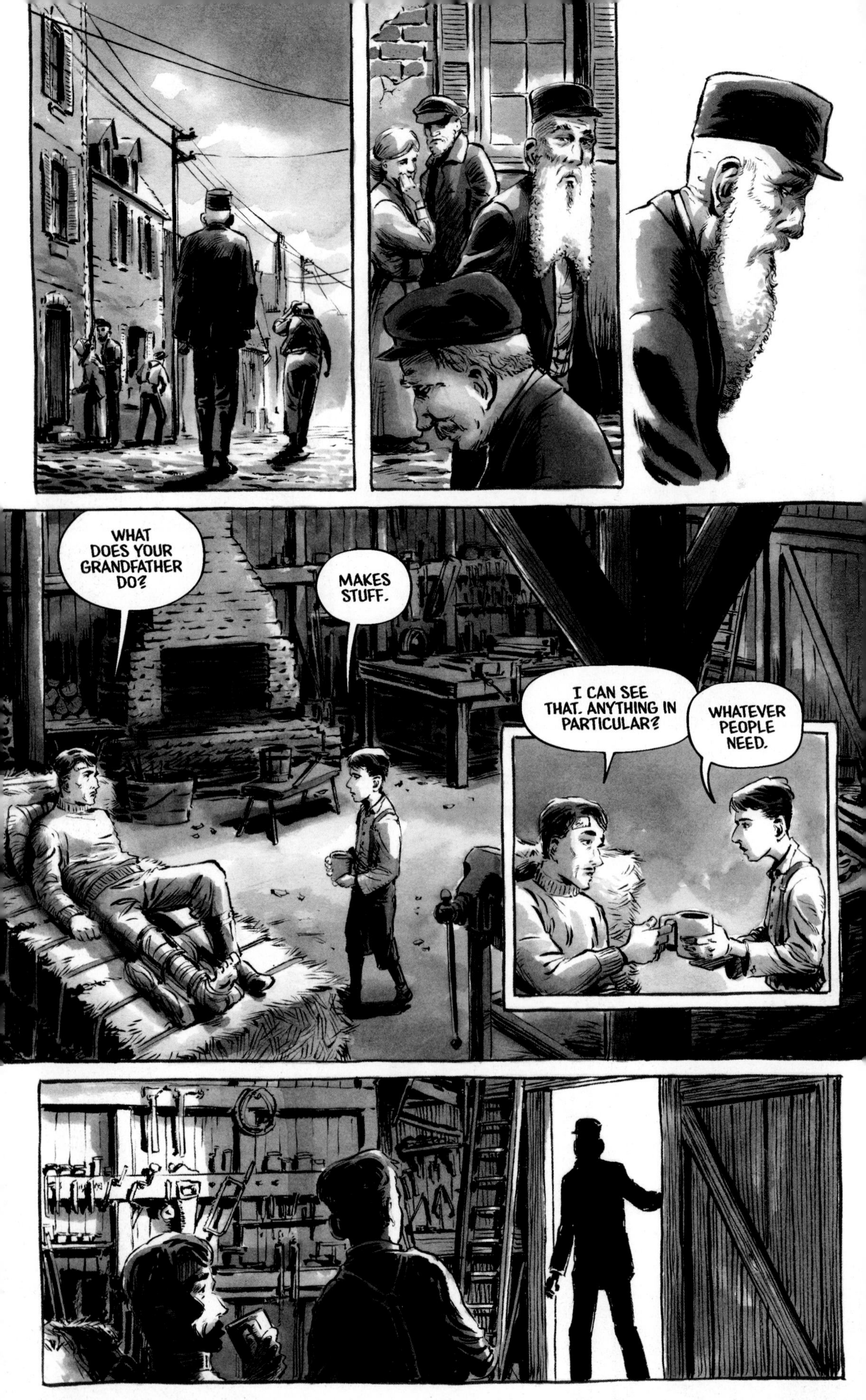
WHAT DOES YOUR GRANDFATHER DO?
MAKES STUFF.
I CAN SEE THAT. ANYTHING IN PARTICULAR?
WHATEVER PEOPLE NEED.

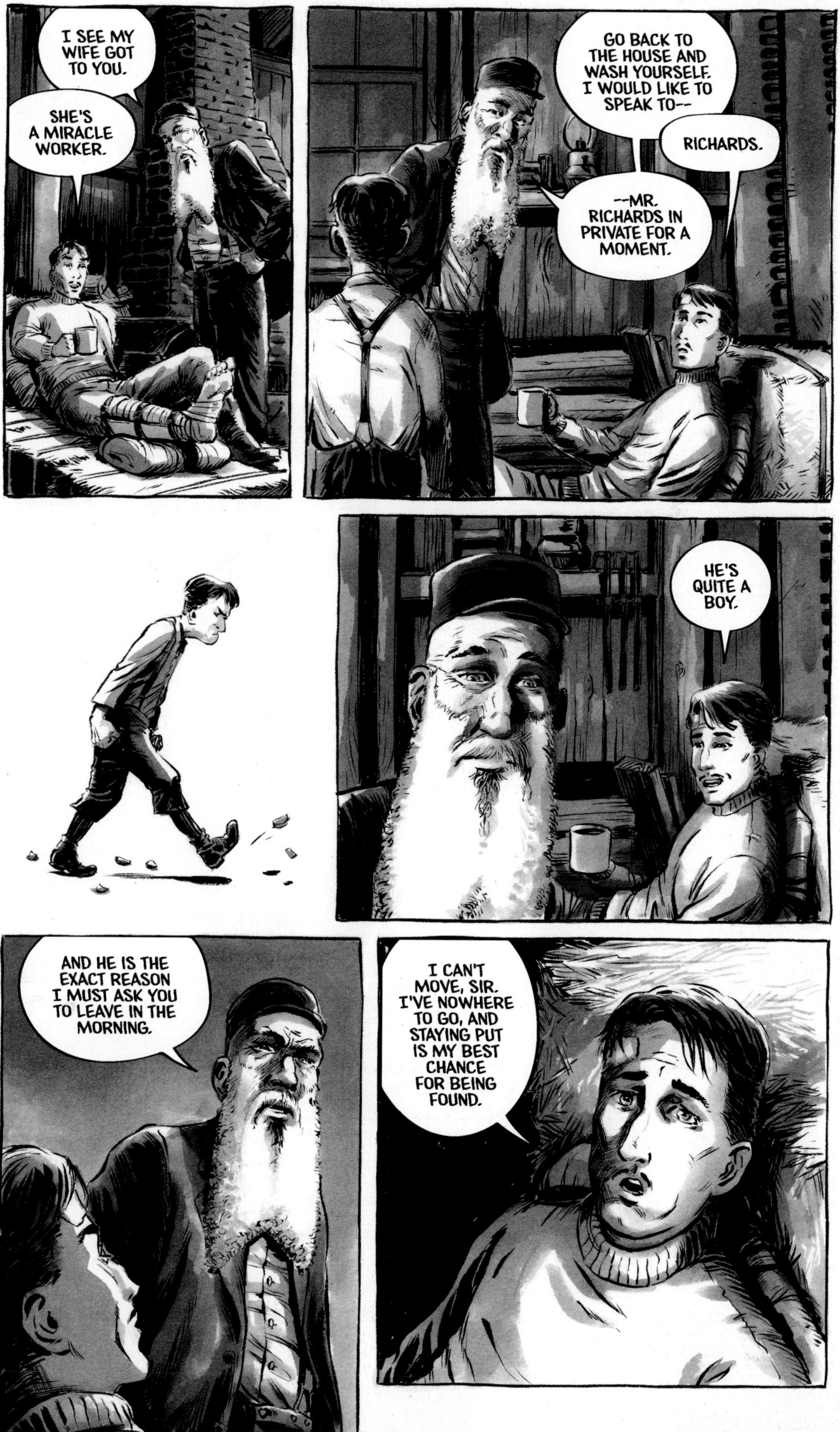
I SEE MY WIFE GOT TO YOU.
SHE'S A MIRACLE WORKER.
GO BACK TO THE HOUSE AND WASH YOURSELF. I WOULD LIKE TO SPEAK TO--
RICHARDS.
--MR. RICHARDS IN PRIVATE FOR A MOMENT.
HE'S QUITE A BOY.
AND HE IS THE EXACT REASON I MUST ASK YOU TO LEAVE IN THE MORNING.
I CAN'T MOVE, SIR. I'VE NOWHERE TO GO, AND STAYING PUT IS MY BEST CHANCE FOR BEING FOUND.

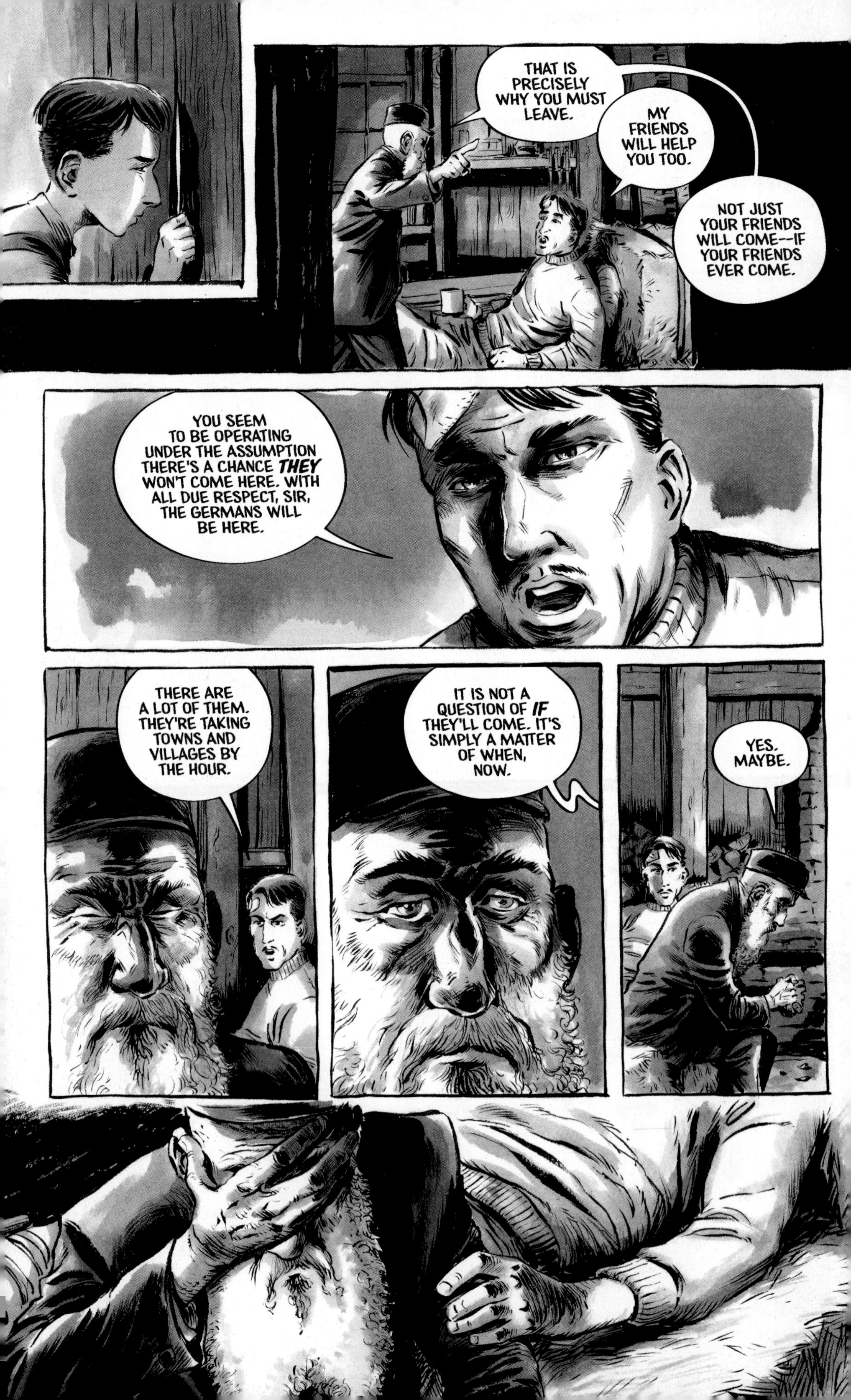
THAT IS PRECISELY WHY YOU MUST LEAVE.
MY FRIENDS WILL HELP YOU TOO.
NOT JUST YOUR FRIENDS WILL COME--IF YOUR FRIENDS EVER COME.
YOU SEEM TO BE OPERATING UNDER THE ASSUMPTION THERE'S A CHANCE *THEY* WON'T COME HERE. WITH ALL DUE RESPECT, SIR, THE GERMANS WILL BE HERE.
THERE ARE A LOT OF THEM. THEY'RE TAKING TOWNS AND VILLAGES BY THE HOUR.
IT IS NOT A QUESTION OF *IF* THEY'LL COME. IT'S SIMPLY A MATTER OF WHEN, NOW.
YES. MAYBE.

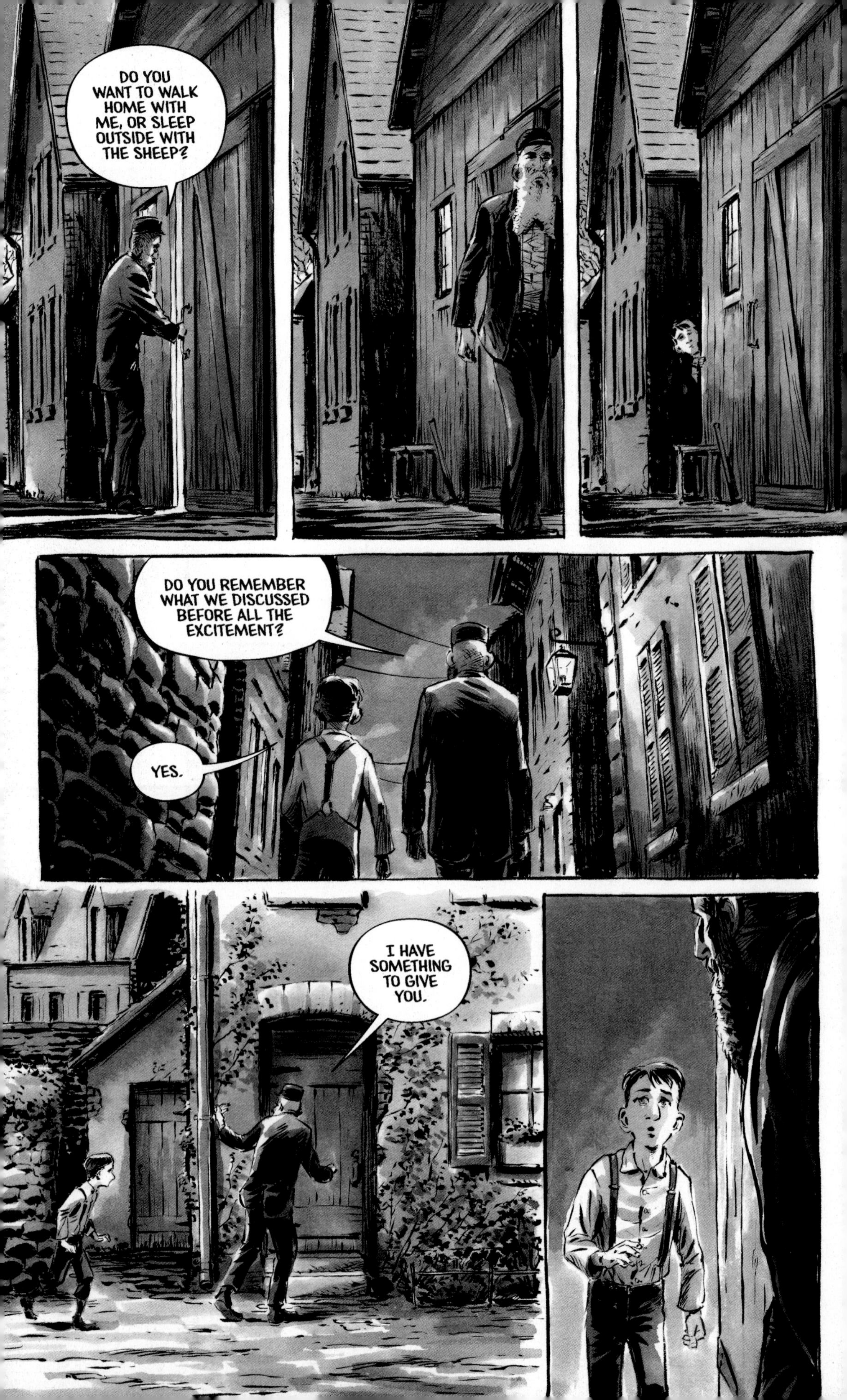
DO YOU WANT TO WALK HOME WITH ME, OR SLEEP OUTSIDE WITH THE SHEEP?
DO YOU REMEMBER WHAT WE DISCUSSED BEFORE ALL THE EXCITEMENT?
YES.
I HAVE SOMETHING TO GIVE YOU.

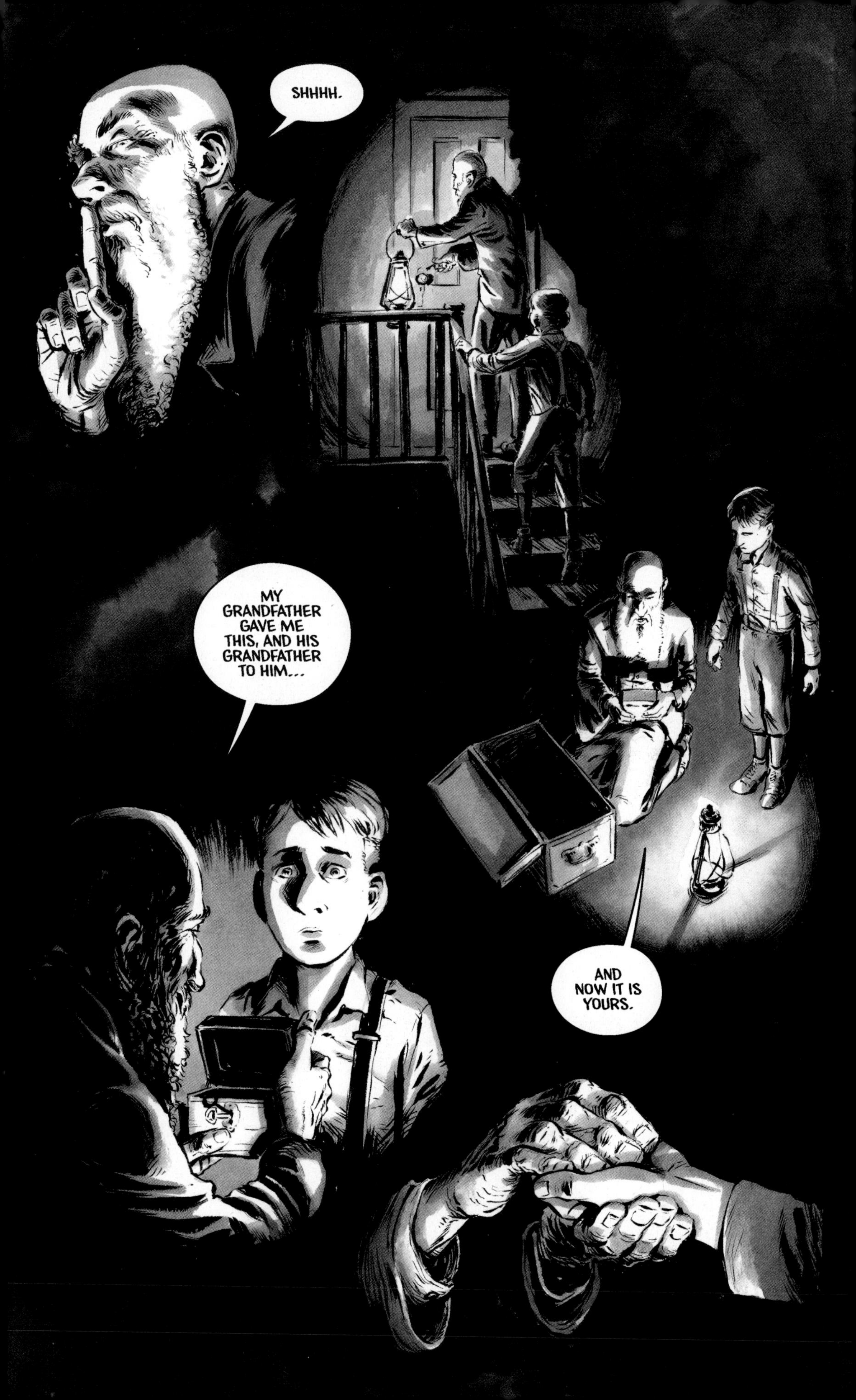
SHHHH.
MY GRANDFATHER GAVE ME THIS, AND HIS GRANDFATHER TO HIM...
AND NOW IT IS YOURS.

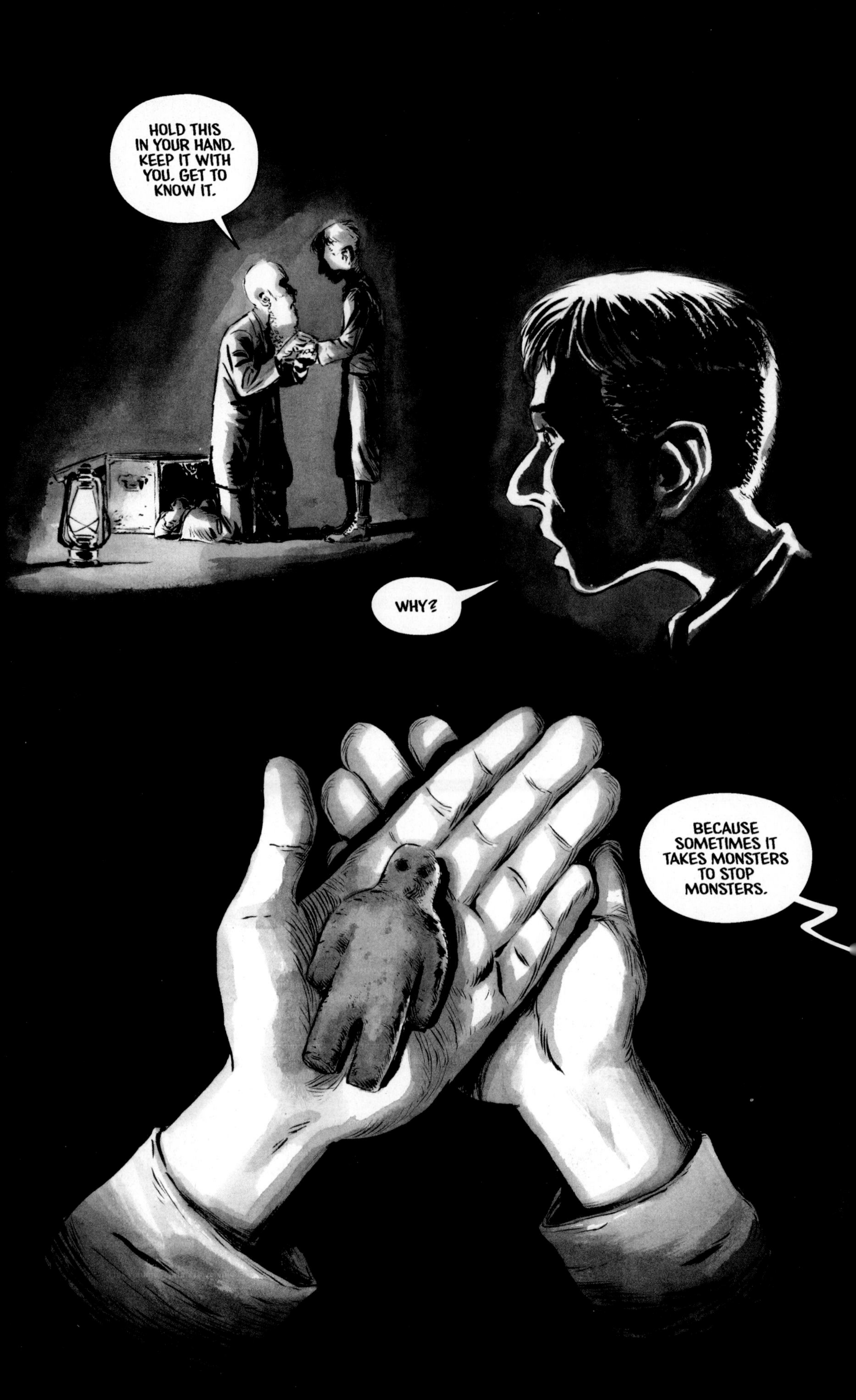
HOLD THIS IN YOUR HAND. KEEP IT WITH YOU. GET TO KNOW IT.
WHY?
BECAUSE SOMETIMES IT TAKES MONSTERS TO STOP MONSTERS.

CHAPTER TWO

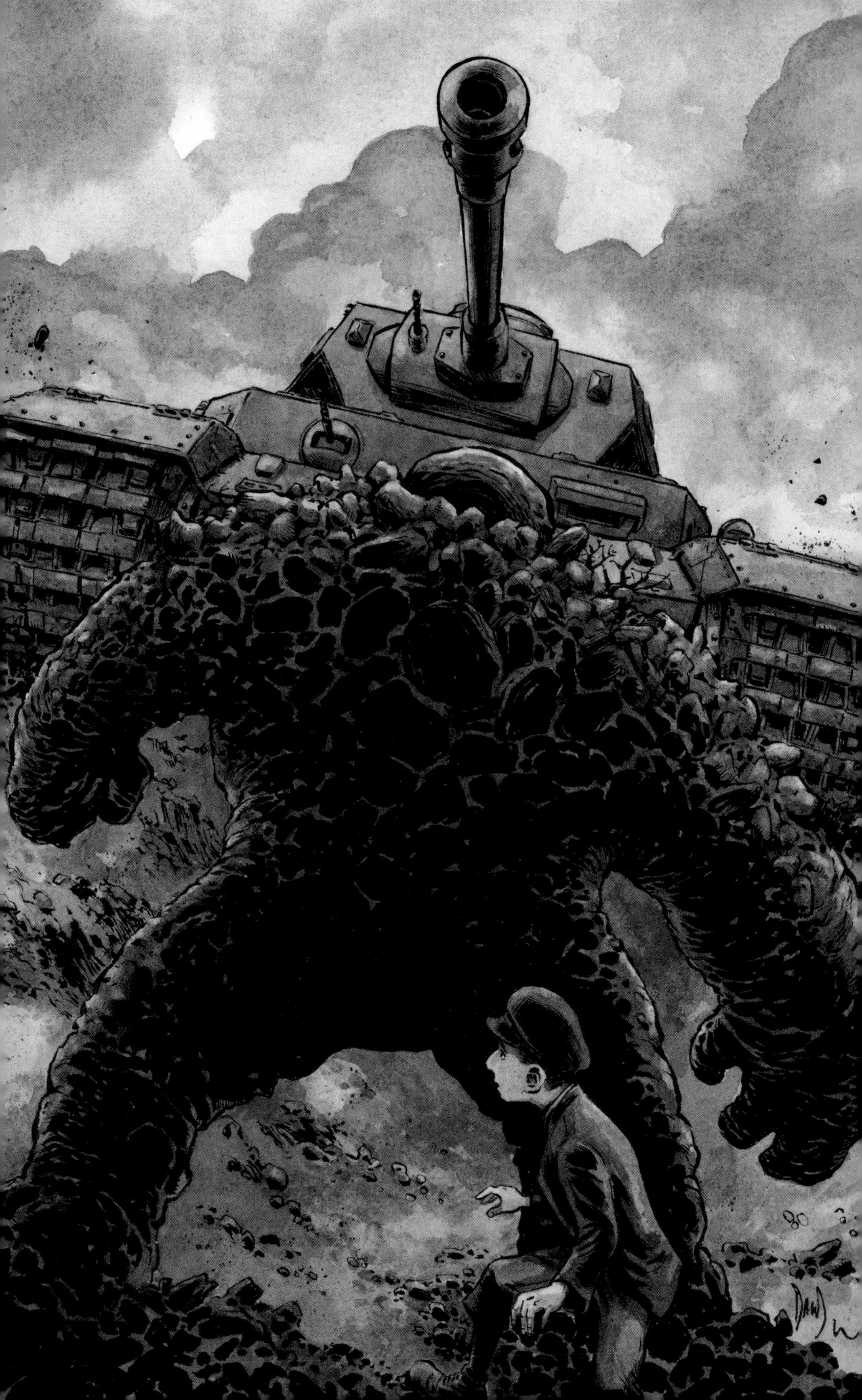

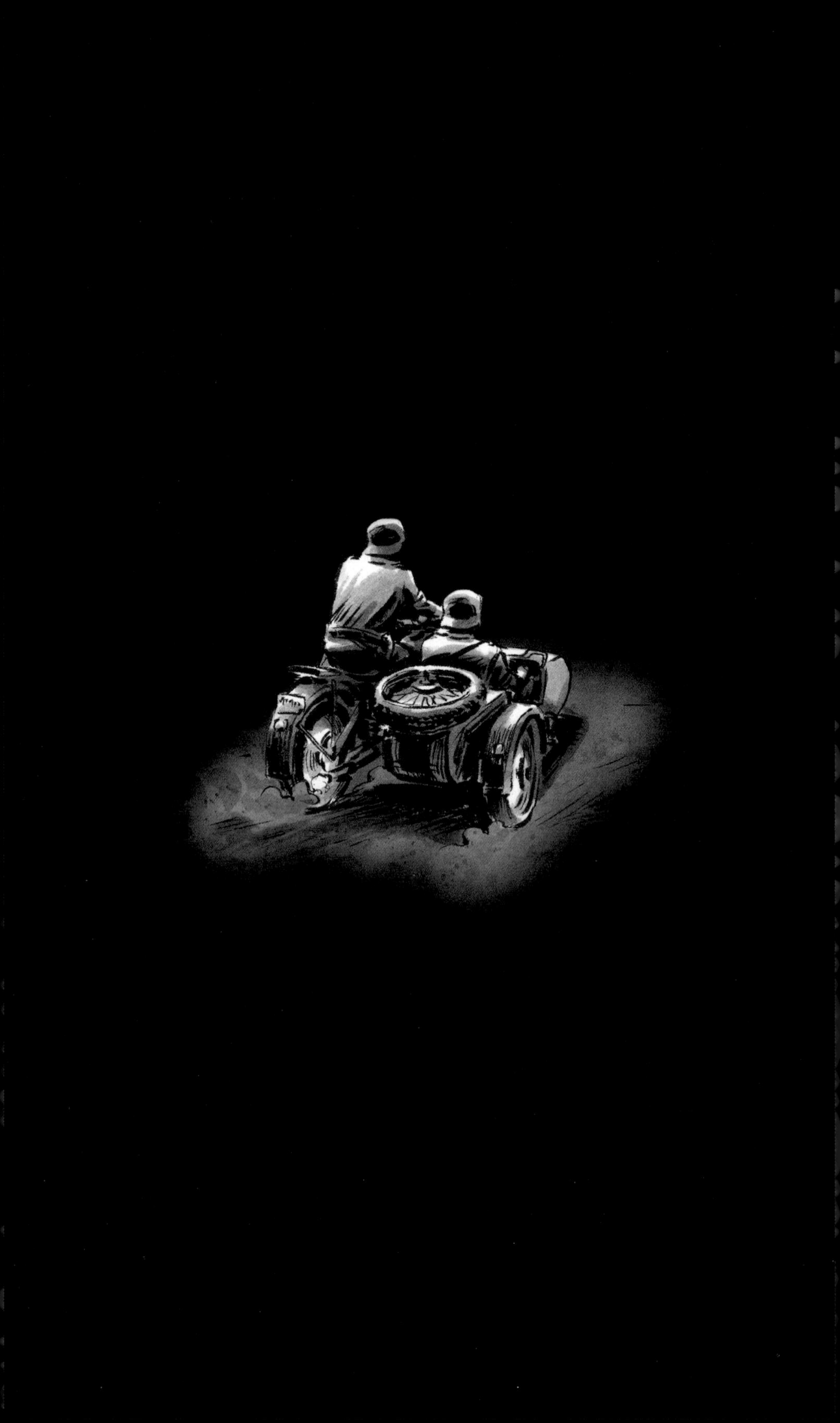

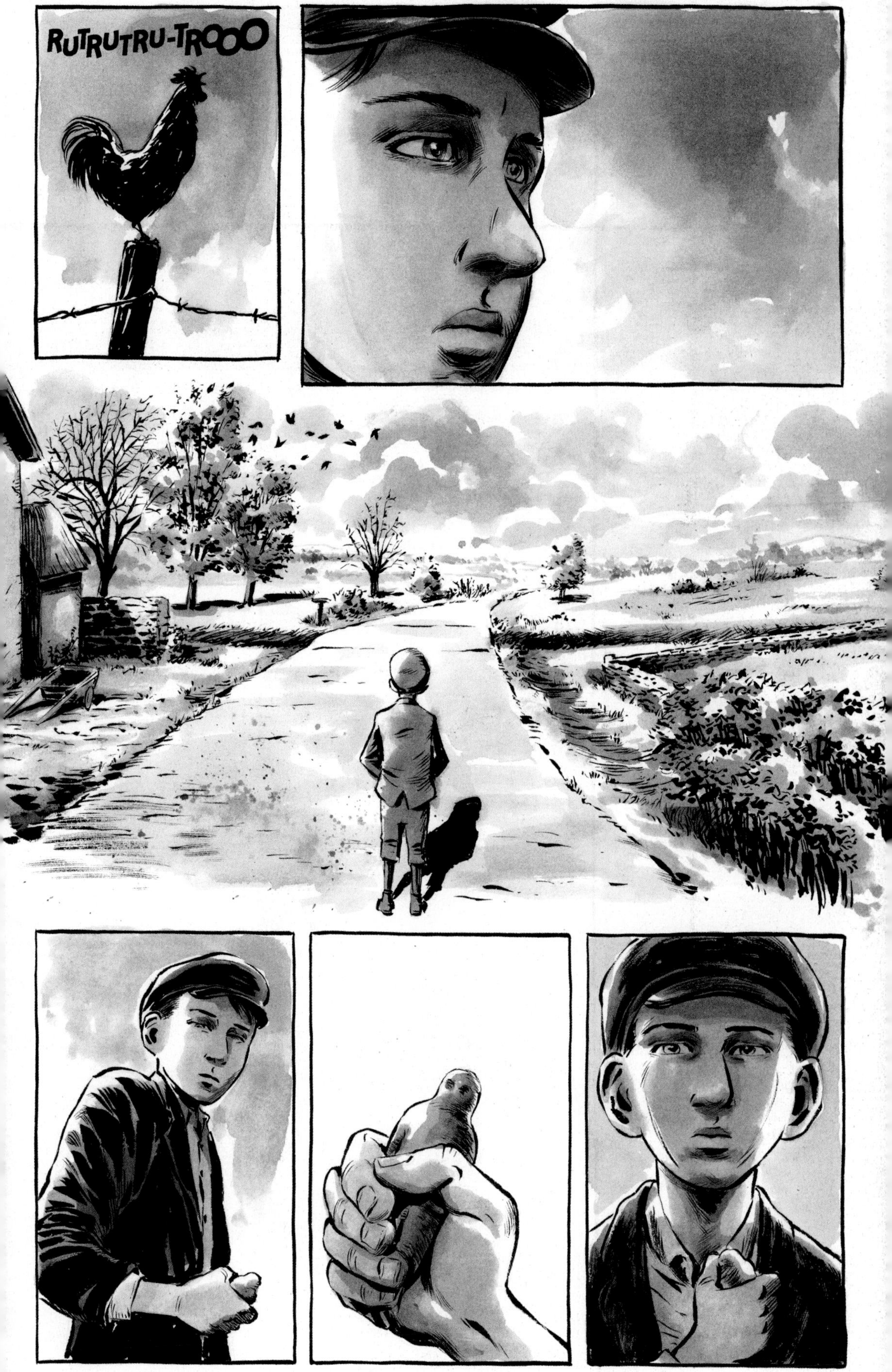
RUTRUTRU-TROOO

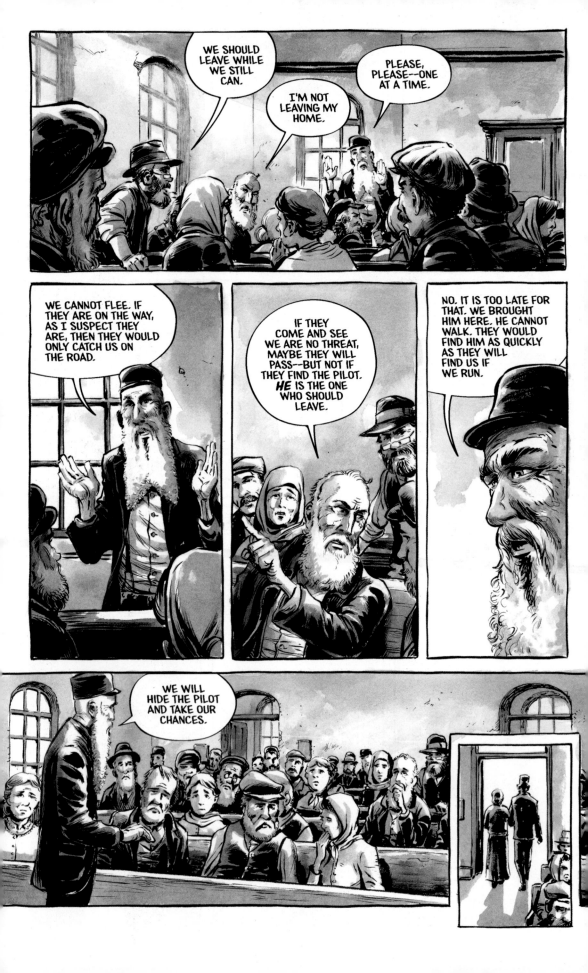

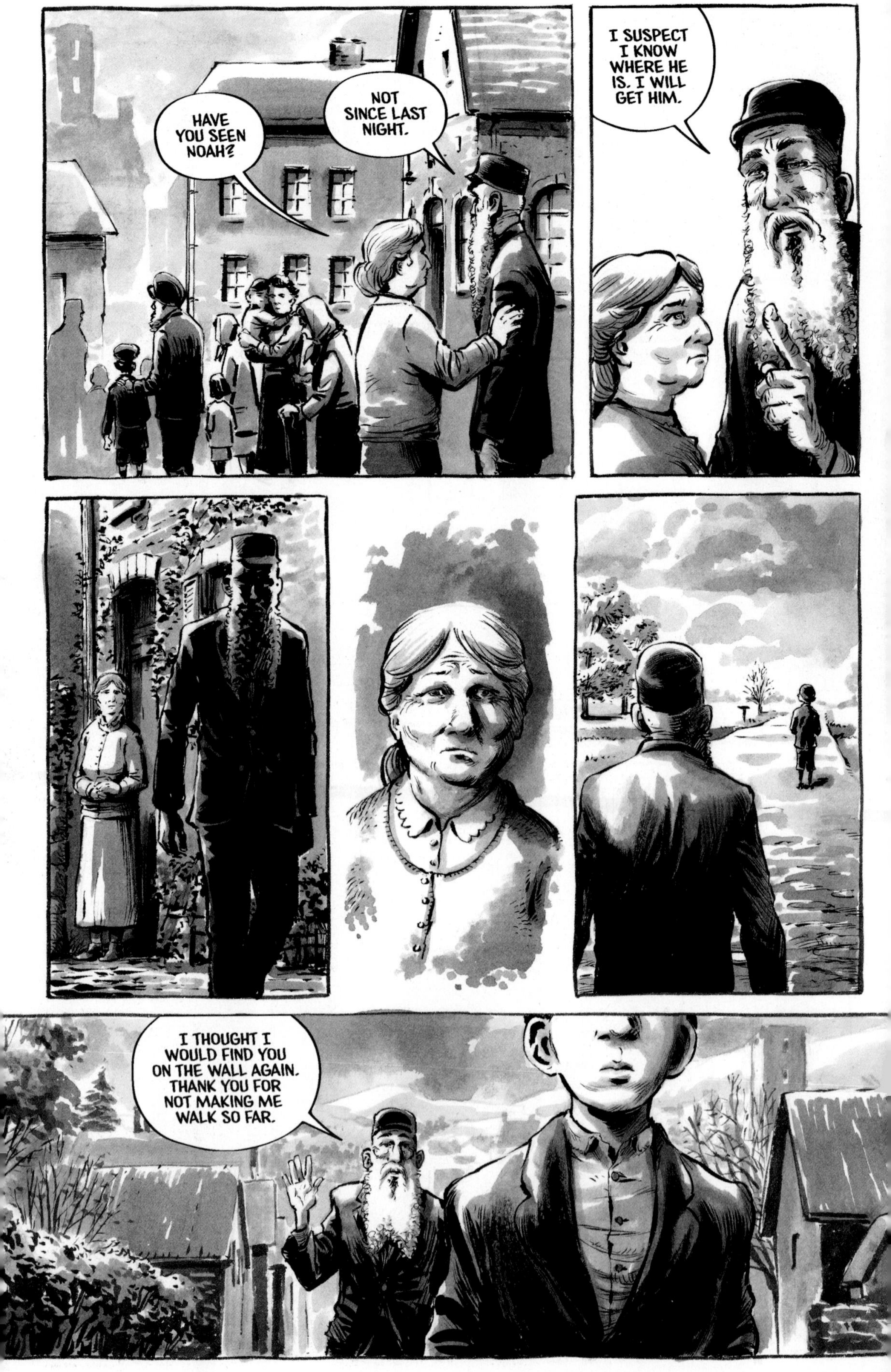
HAVE YOU SEEN NOAH?
NOT SINCE LAST NIGHT.
I SUSPECT I KNOW WHERE HE IS. I WILL GET HIM.
I THOUGHT I WOULD FIND YOU ON THE WALL AGAIN. THANK YOU FOR NOT MAKING ME WALK SO FAR.

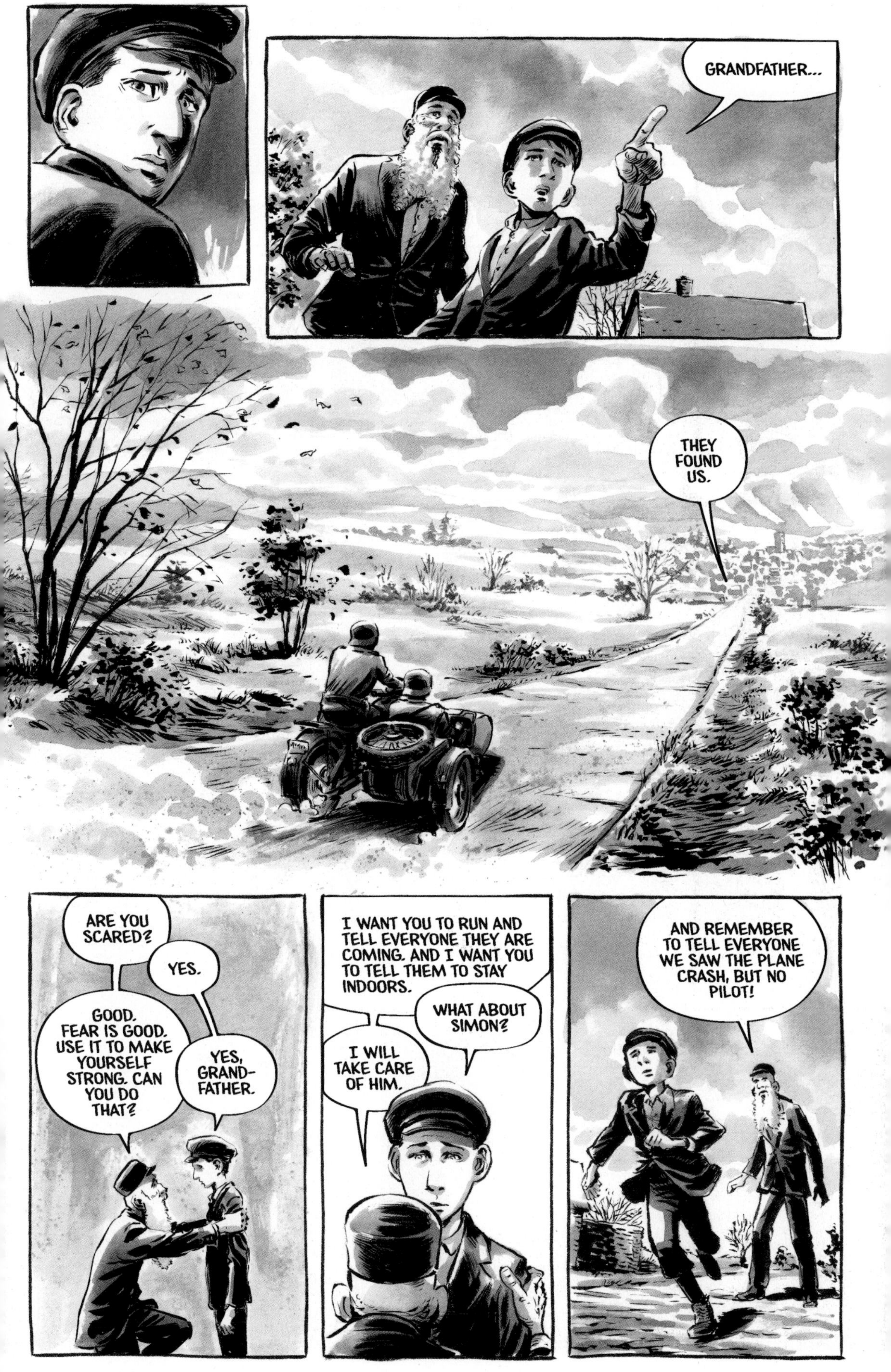
GRANDFATHER...
THEY FOUND US.
ARE YOU SCARED?
YES.
GOOD. FEAR IS GOOD. USE IT TO MAKE YOURSELF STRONG. CAN YOU DO THAT?
YES, GRANDFATHER.
I WANT YOU TO RUN AND TELL EVERYONE THEY ARE COMING. AND I WANT YOU TO TELL THEM TO STAY INDOORS.
WHAT ABOUT SIMON?
I WILL TAKE CARE OF HIM.
AND REMEMBER TO TELL EVERYONE WE SAW THE PLANE CRASH, BUT NO PILOT!

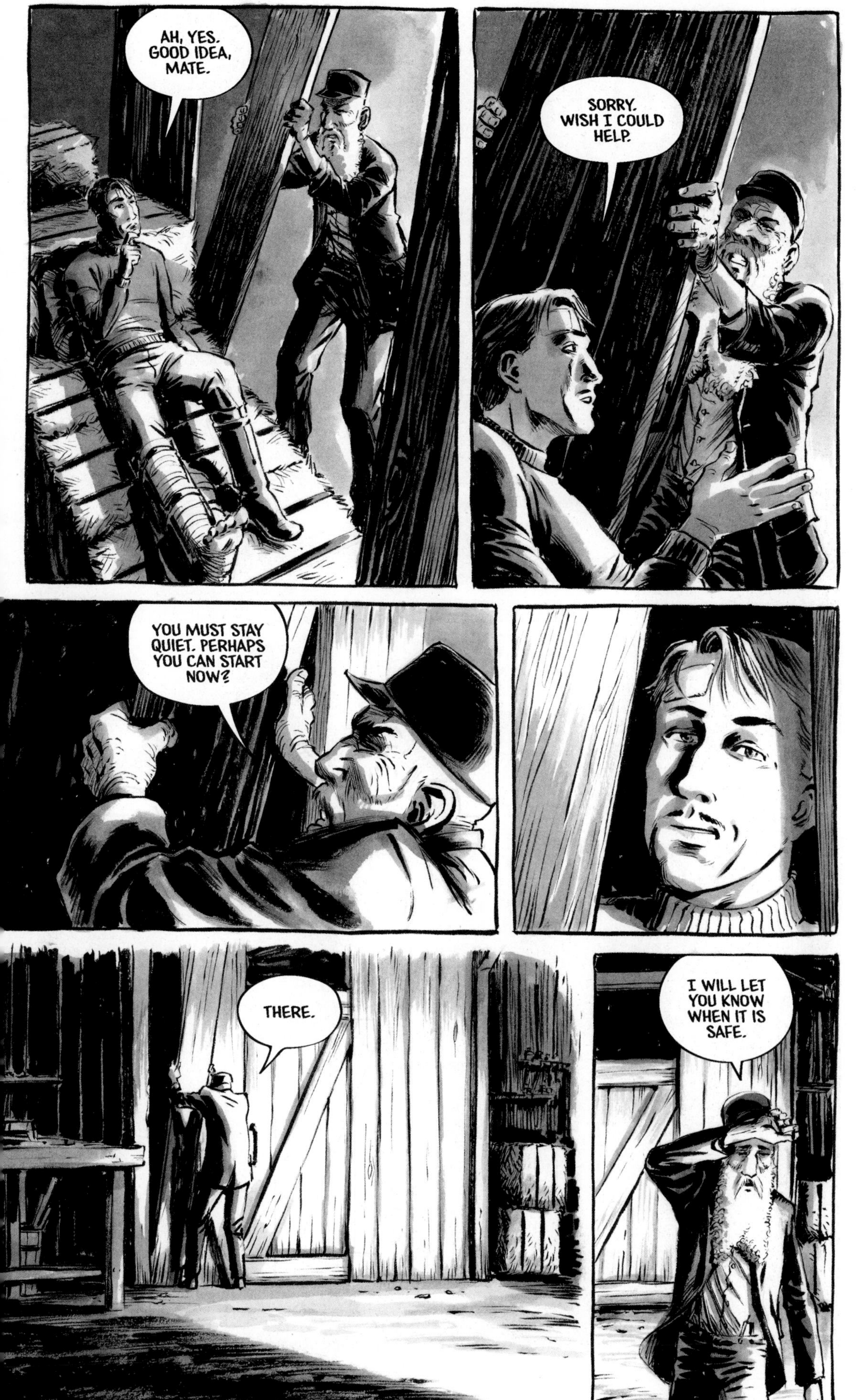
AH, YES. GOOD IDEA, MATE.
SORRY. WISH I COULD HELP.
YOU MUST STAY QUIET. PERHAPS YOU CAN START NOW?
THERE.
I WILL LET YOU KNOW WHEN IT IS SAFE.

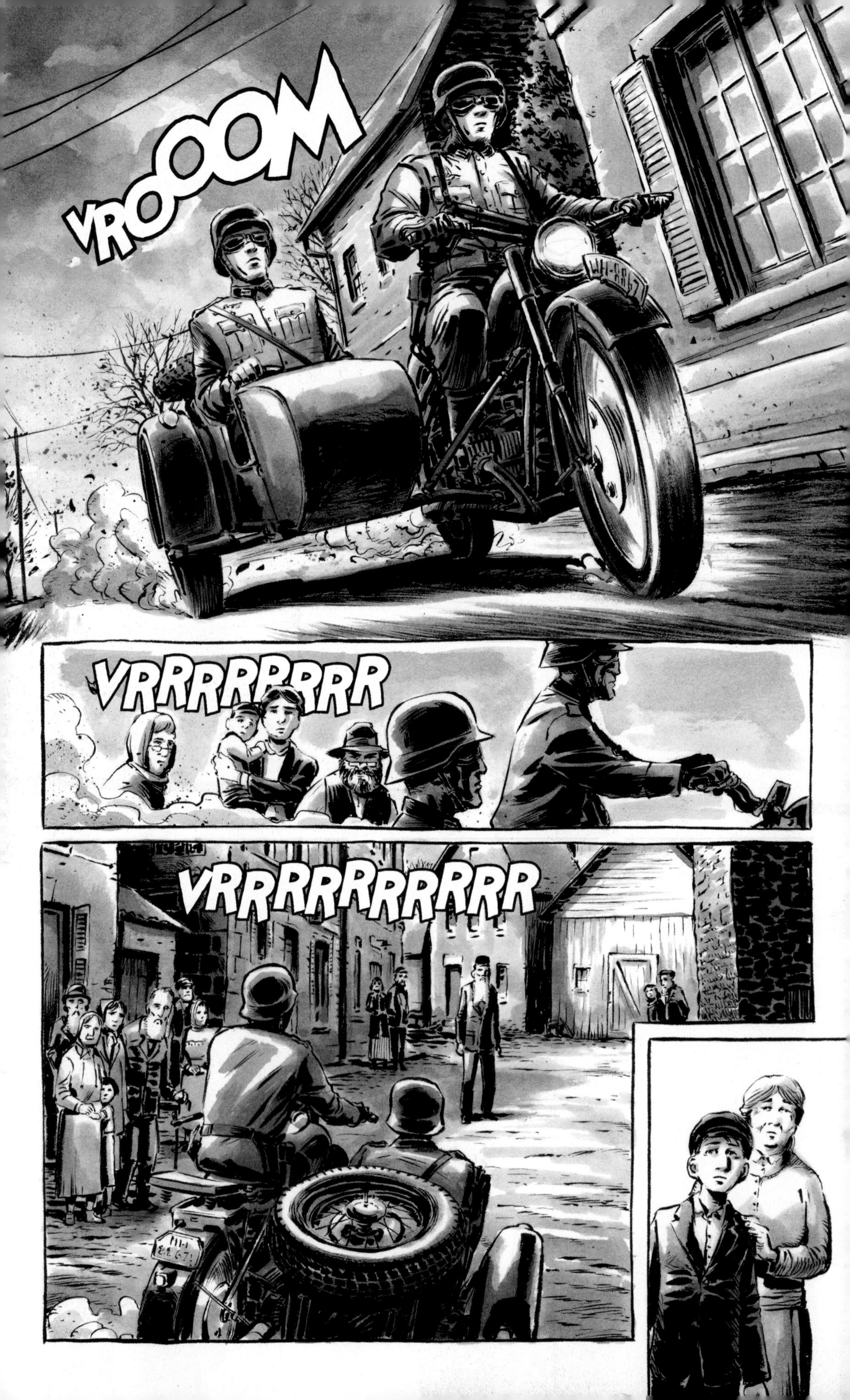
VROOOOM
VRRRRRRRR
VRRRRRRRRRRR

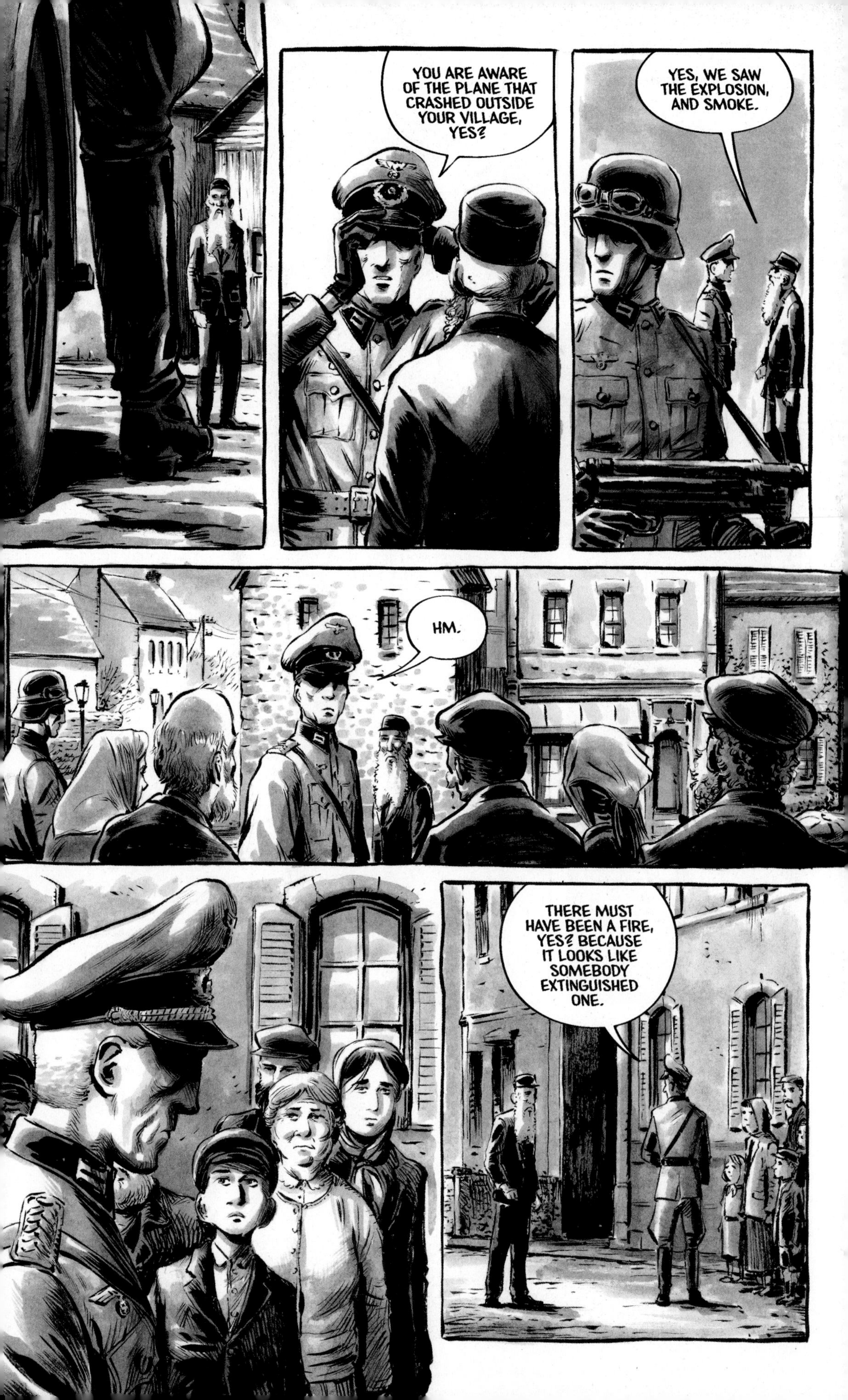
YOU ARE AWARE OF THE PLANE THAT CRASHED OUTSIDE YOUR VILLAGE, YES?
YES, WE SAW THE EXPLOSION, AND SMOKE.
HM.
THERE MUST HAVE BEEN A FIRE, YES? BECAUSE IT LOOKS LIKE SOMEBODY EXTINGUISHED ONE.

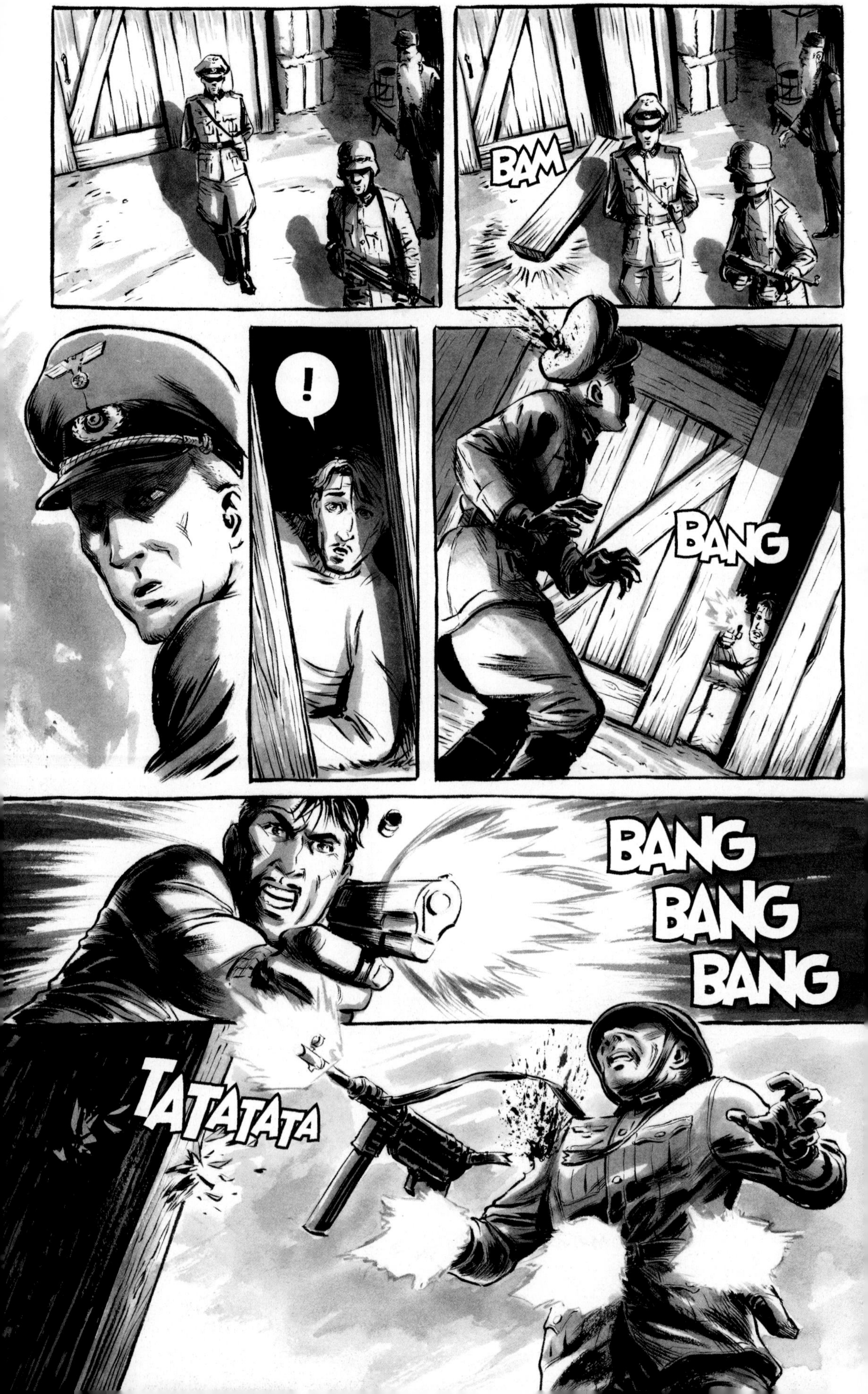
BAM
!
BANG
BANG
BANG
BANG
TATATATA

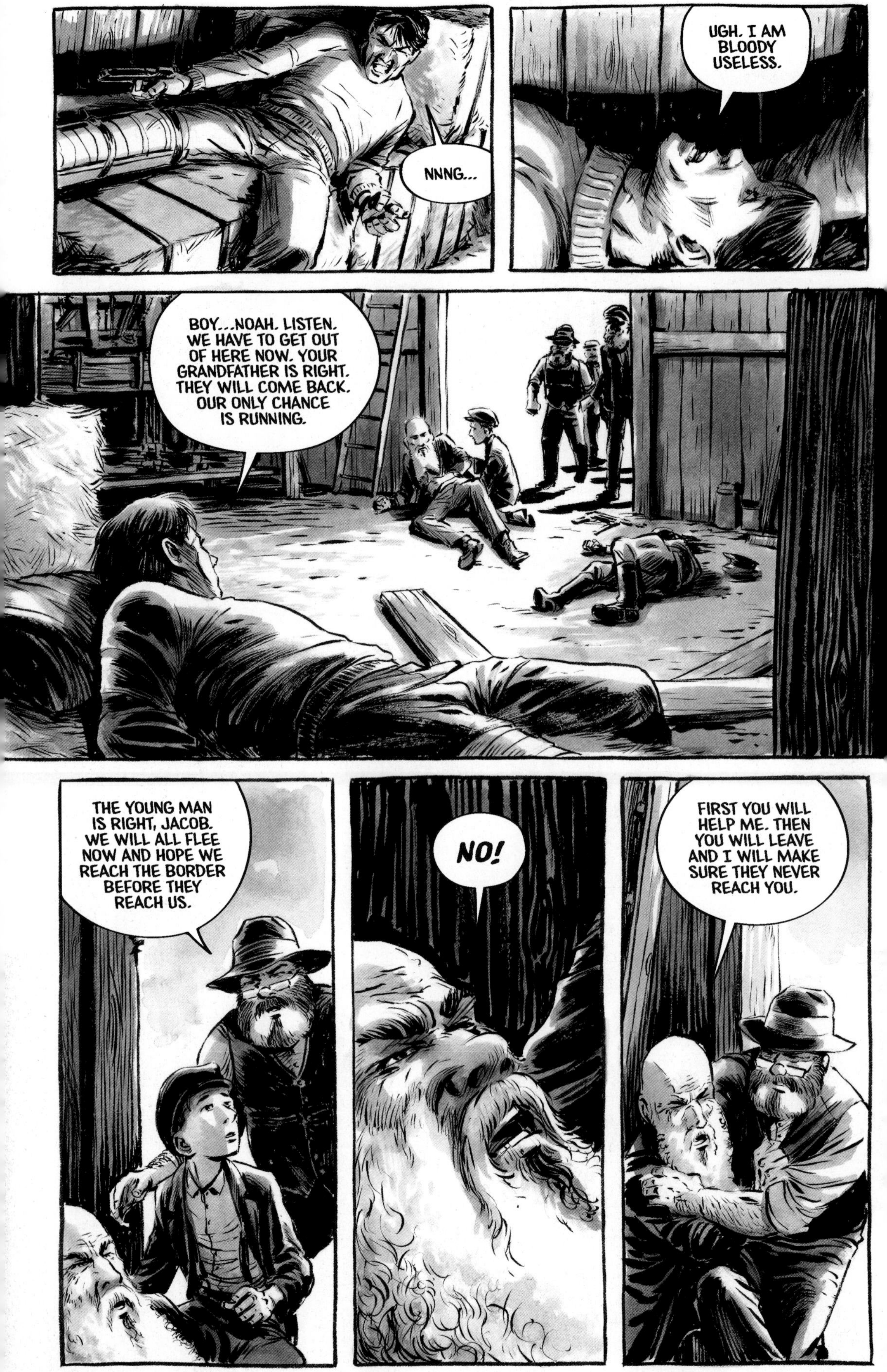
NNNG...
UGH. I AM BLOODY USELESS.
BOY...NOAH. LISTEN. WE HAVE TO GET OUT OF HERE NOW. YOUR GRANDFATHER IS RIGHT. THEY WILL COME BACK. OUR ONLY CHANCE IS RUNNING.
THE YOUNG MAN IS RIGHT, JACOB. WE WILL ALL FLEE NOW AND HOPE WE REACH THE BORDER BEFORE THEY REACH US.
NO!
FIRST YOU WILL HELP ME. THEN YOU WILL LEAVE AND I WILL MAKE SURE THEY NEVER REACH YOU.

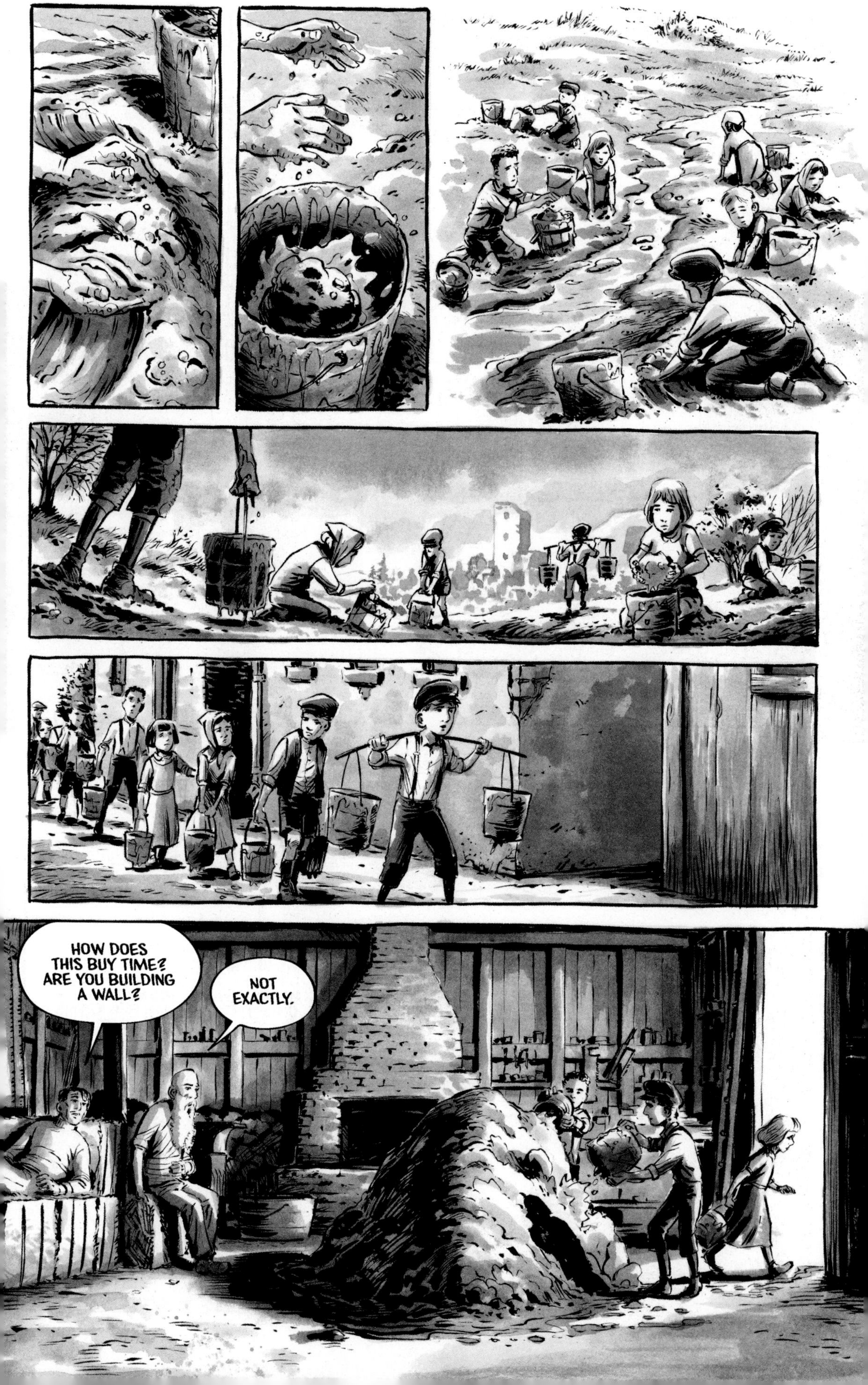
HOW DOES THIS BUY TIME? ARE YOU BUILDING A WALL?
NOT EXACTLY.

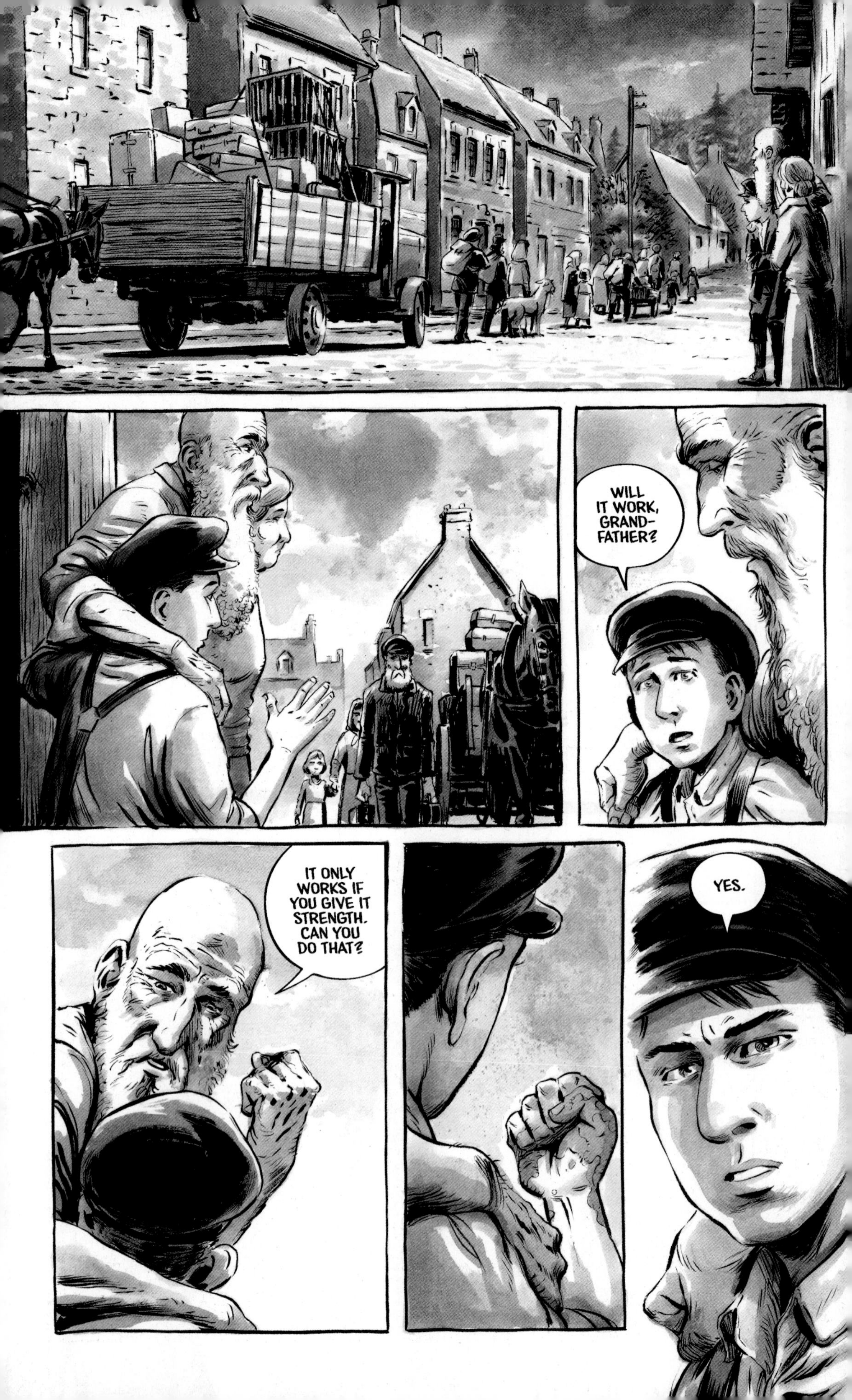
WILL IT WORK, GRAND-FATHER?
IT ONLY WORKS IF YOU GIVE IT STRENGTH. CAN YOU DO THAT?
YES.

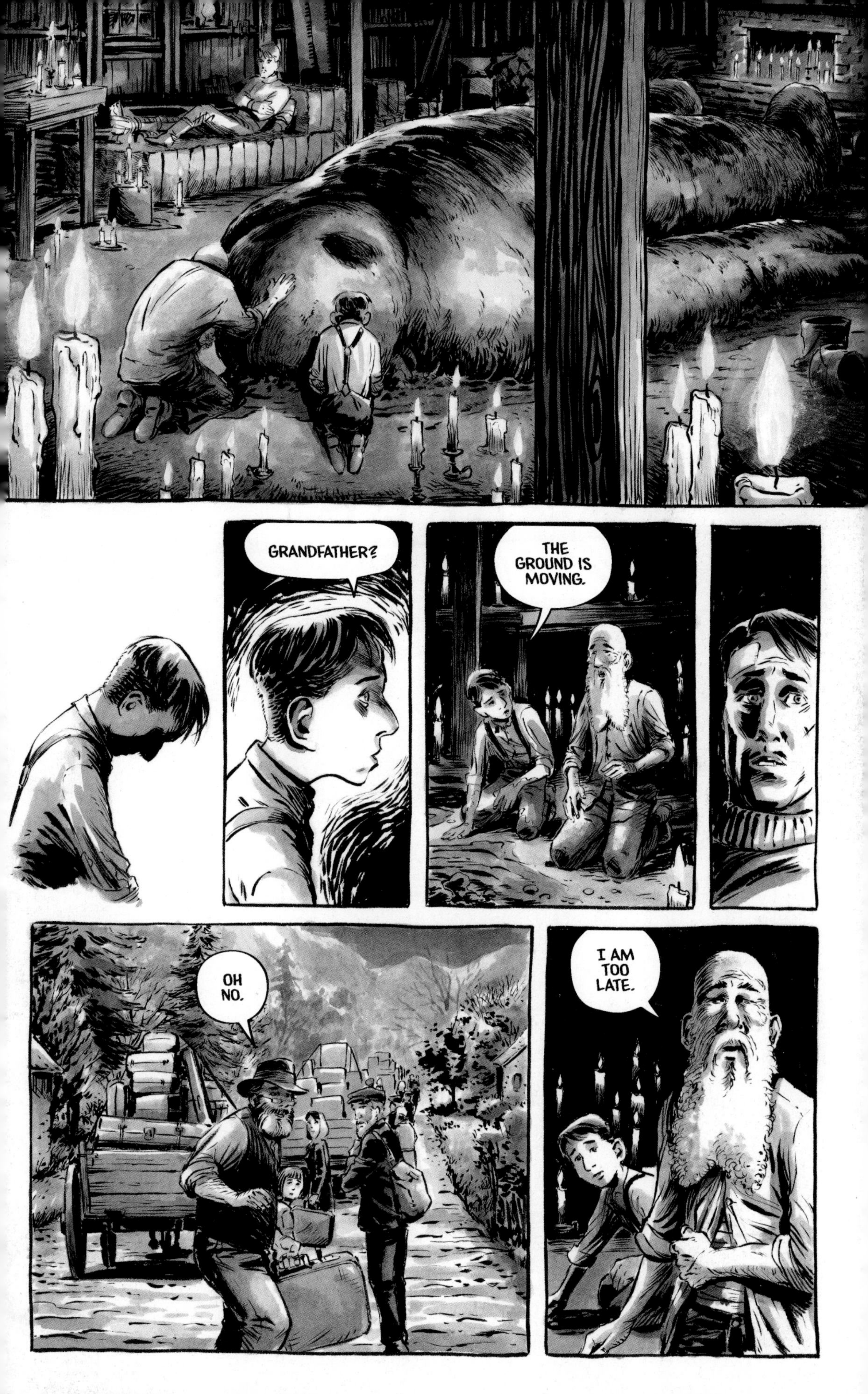
GRANDFATHER?
THE GROUND IS MOVING.
OH NO.
I AM TOO LATE.

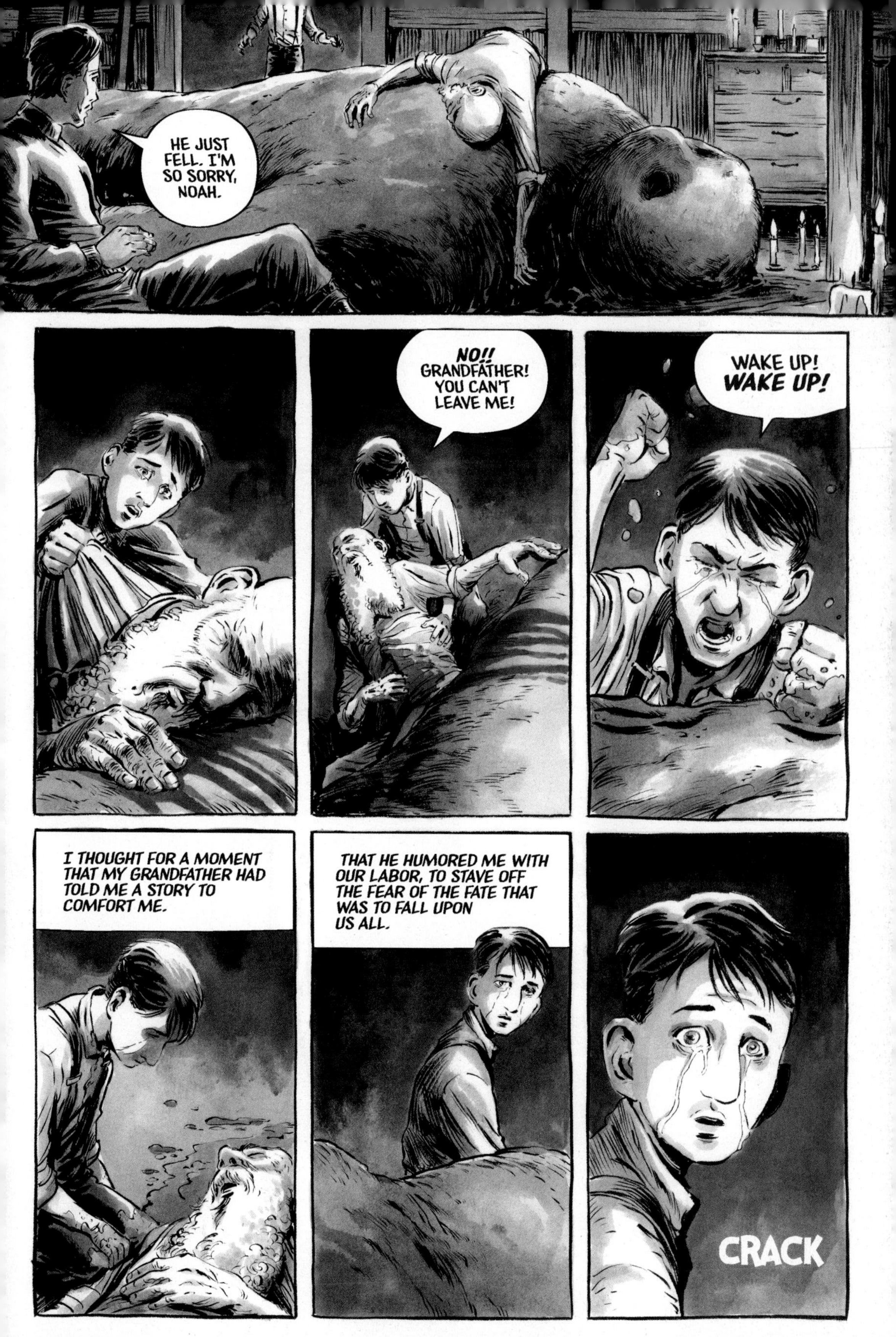
HE JUST FELL. I'M SO SORRY, NOAH.
NO!! GRANDFATHER! YOU CAN'T LEAVE ME!
WAKE UP! WAKE UP!
I THOUGHT FOR A MOMENT THAT MY GRANDFATHER HAD TOLD ME A STORY TO COMFORT ME.
THAT HE HUMORED ME WITH OUR LABOR, TO STAVE OFF THE FEAR OF THE FATE THAT WAS TO FALL UPON US ALL.
CRACK

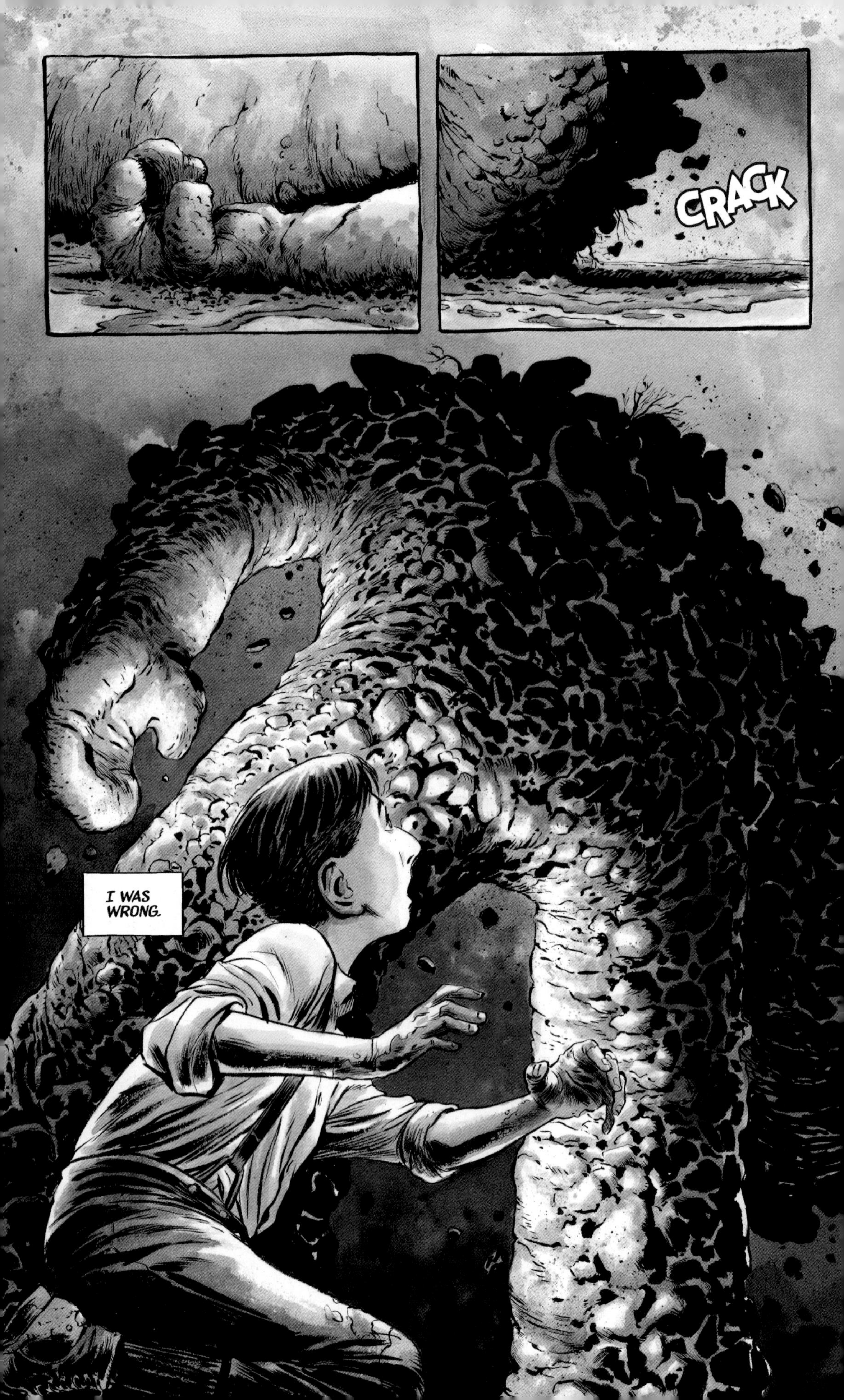
CRACK
I WAS WRONG.

CHAPTER THREE

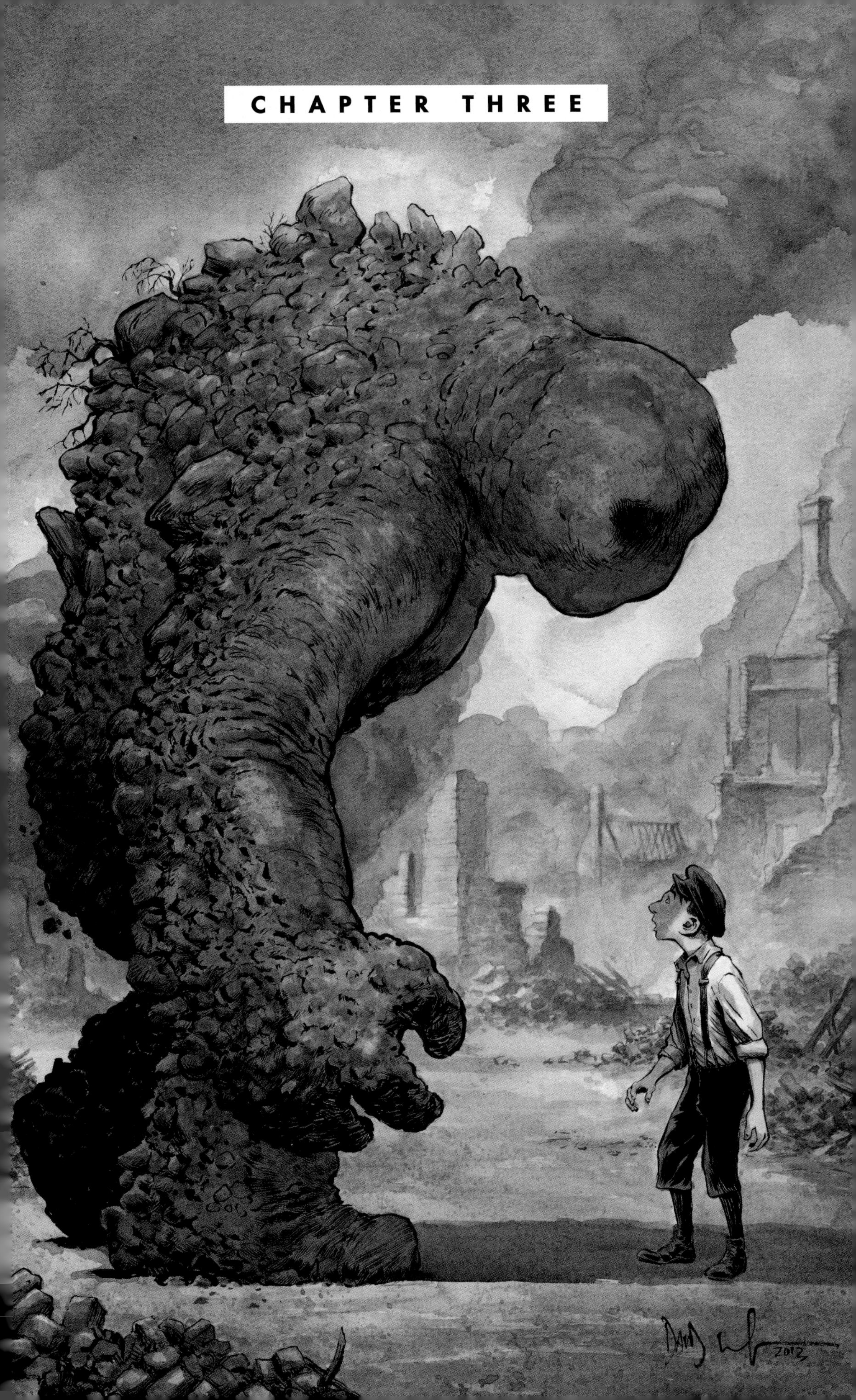

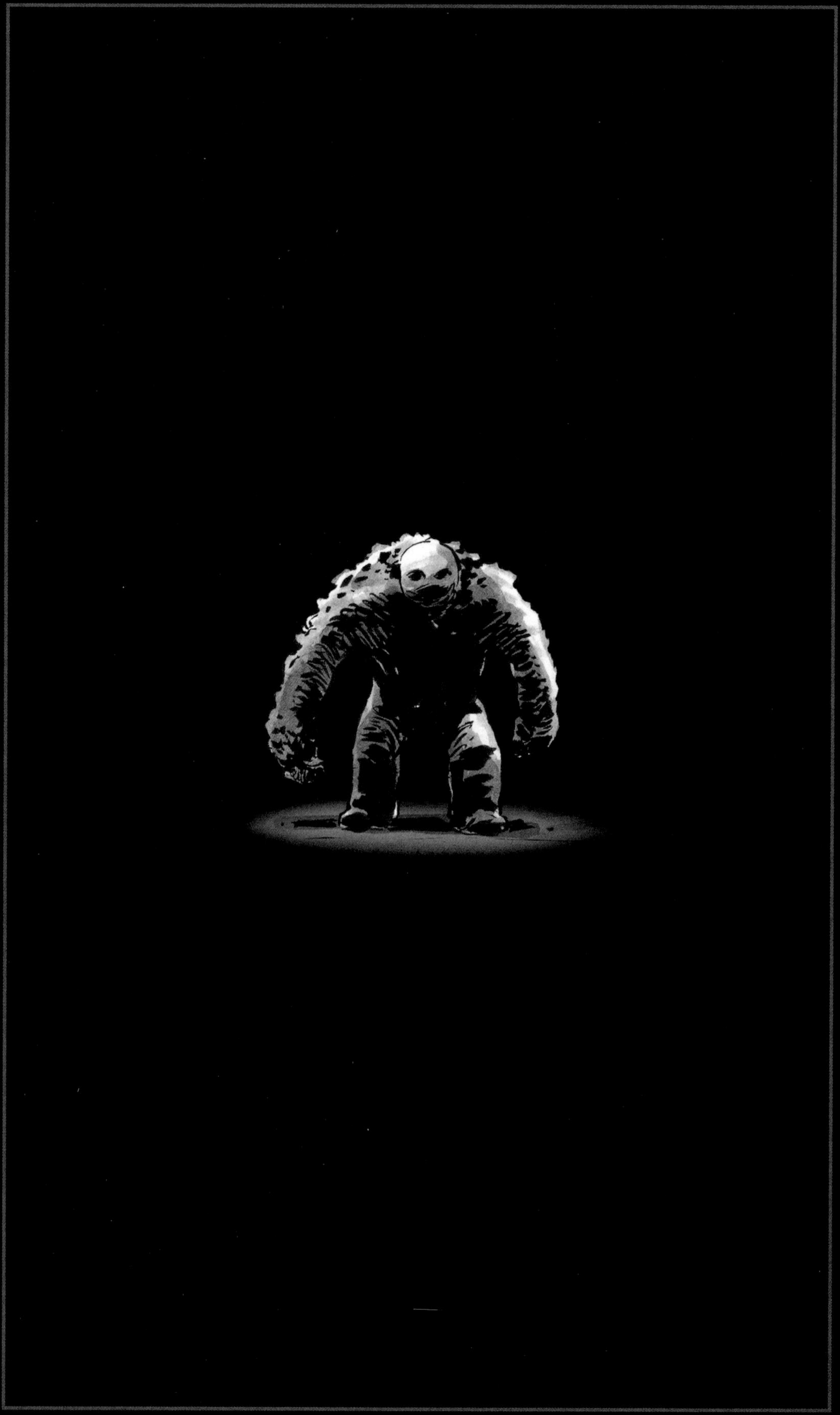

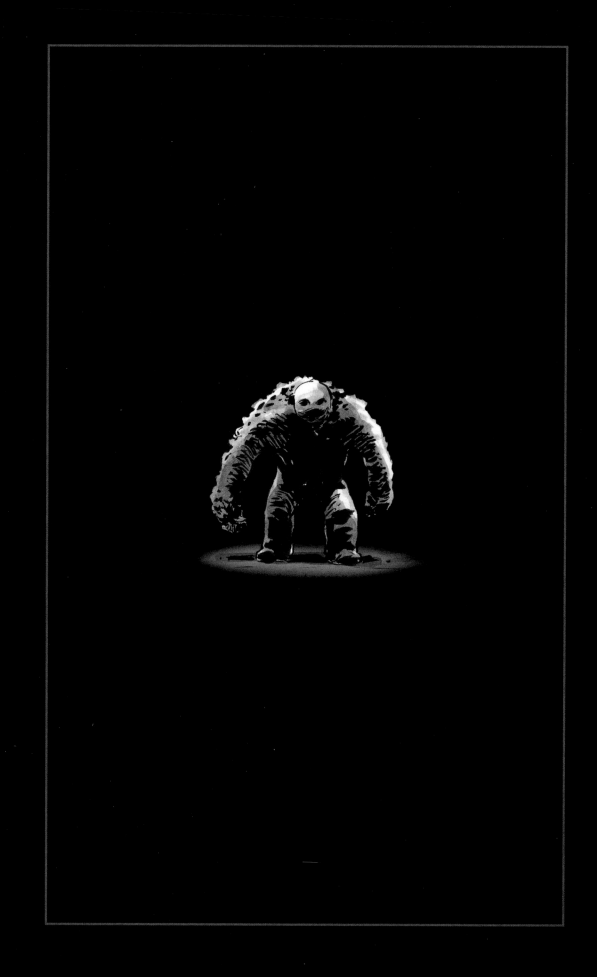

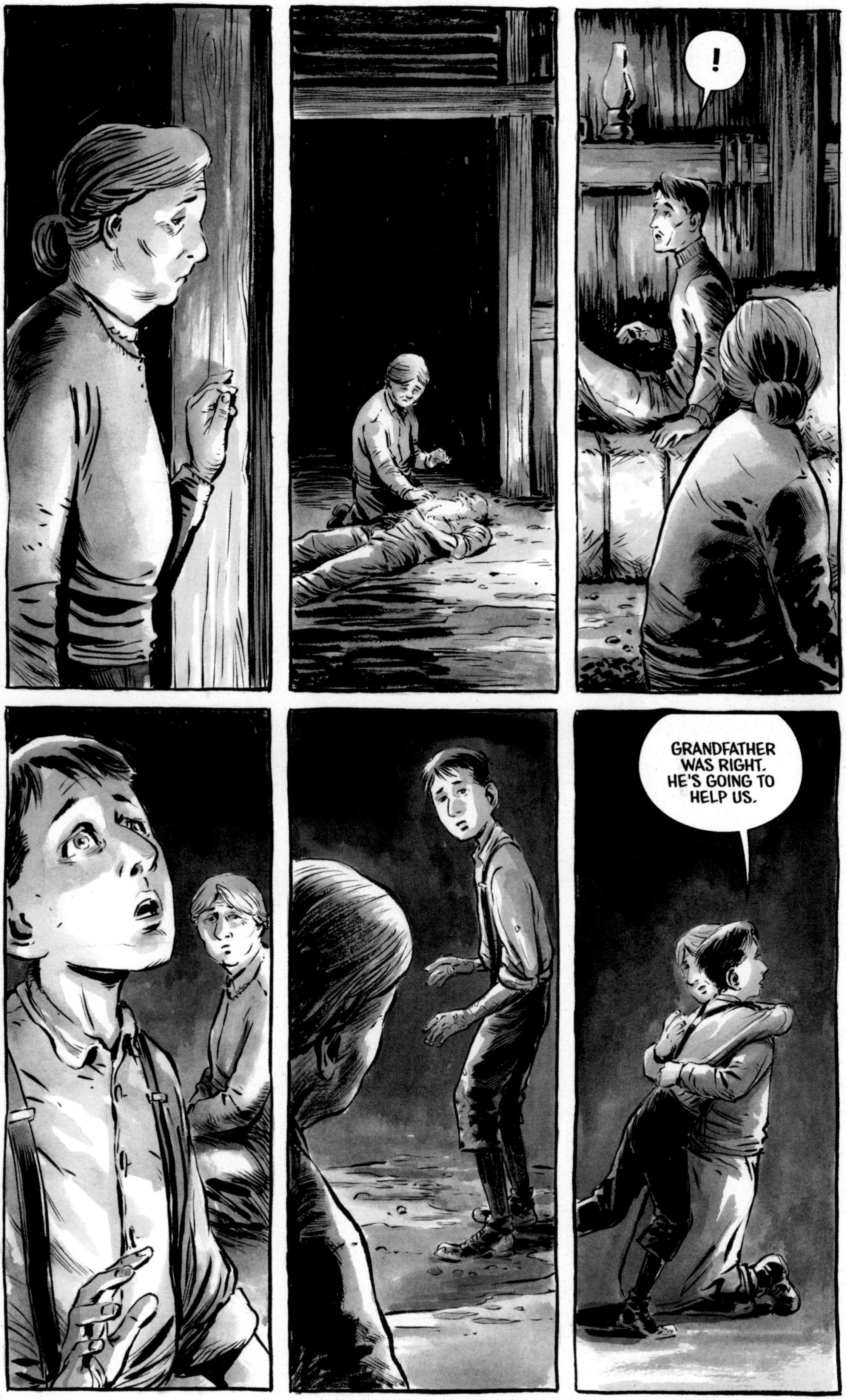
!
GRANDFATHER WAS RIGHT. HE'S GOING TO HELP US.

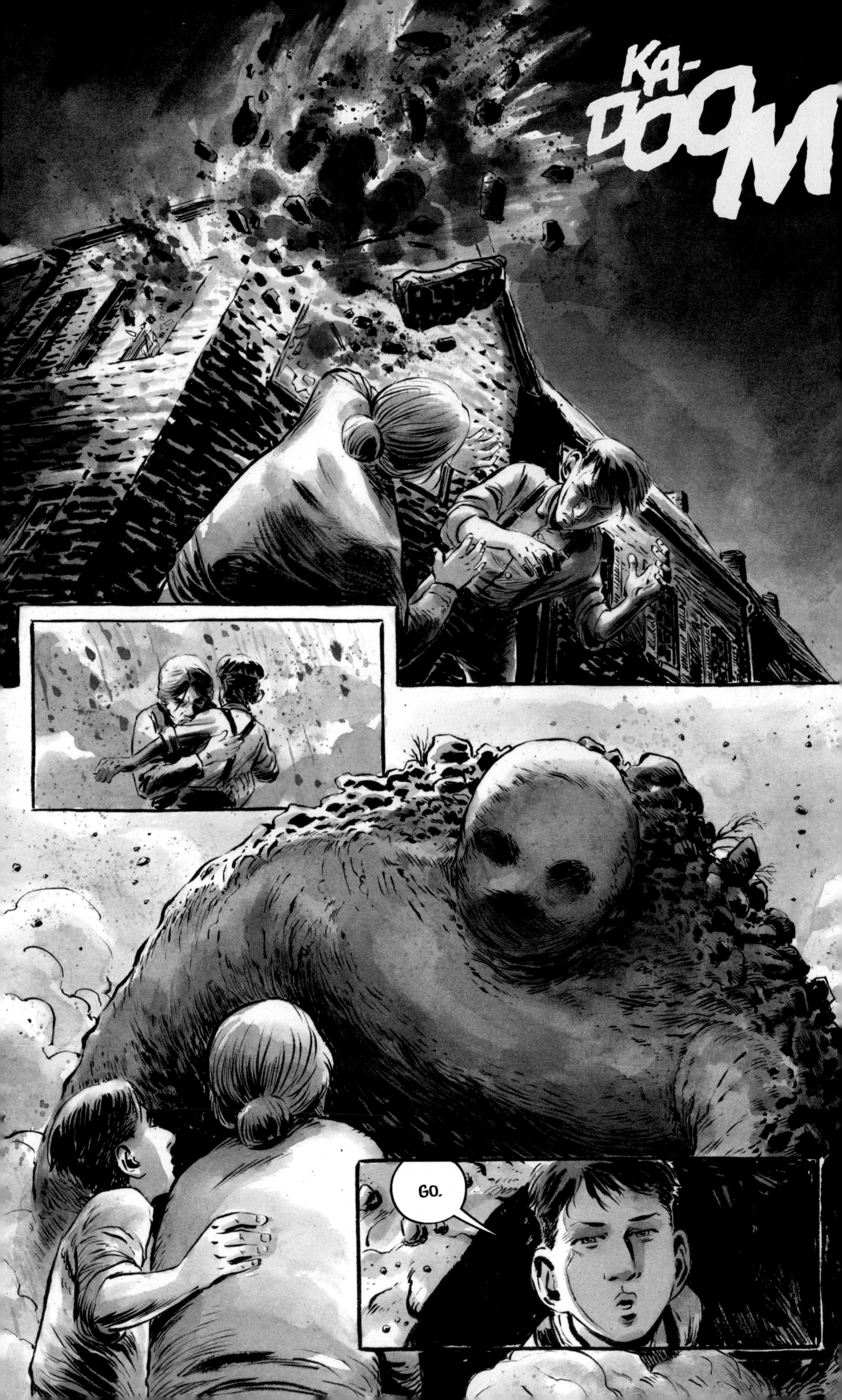
KA-
DOOM
GO.

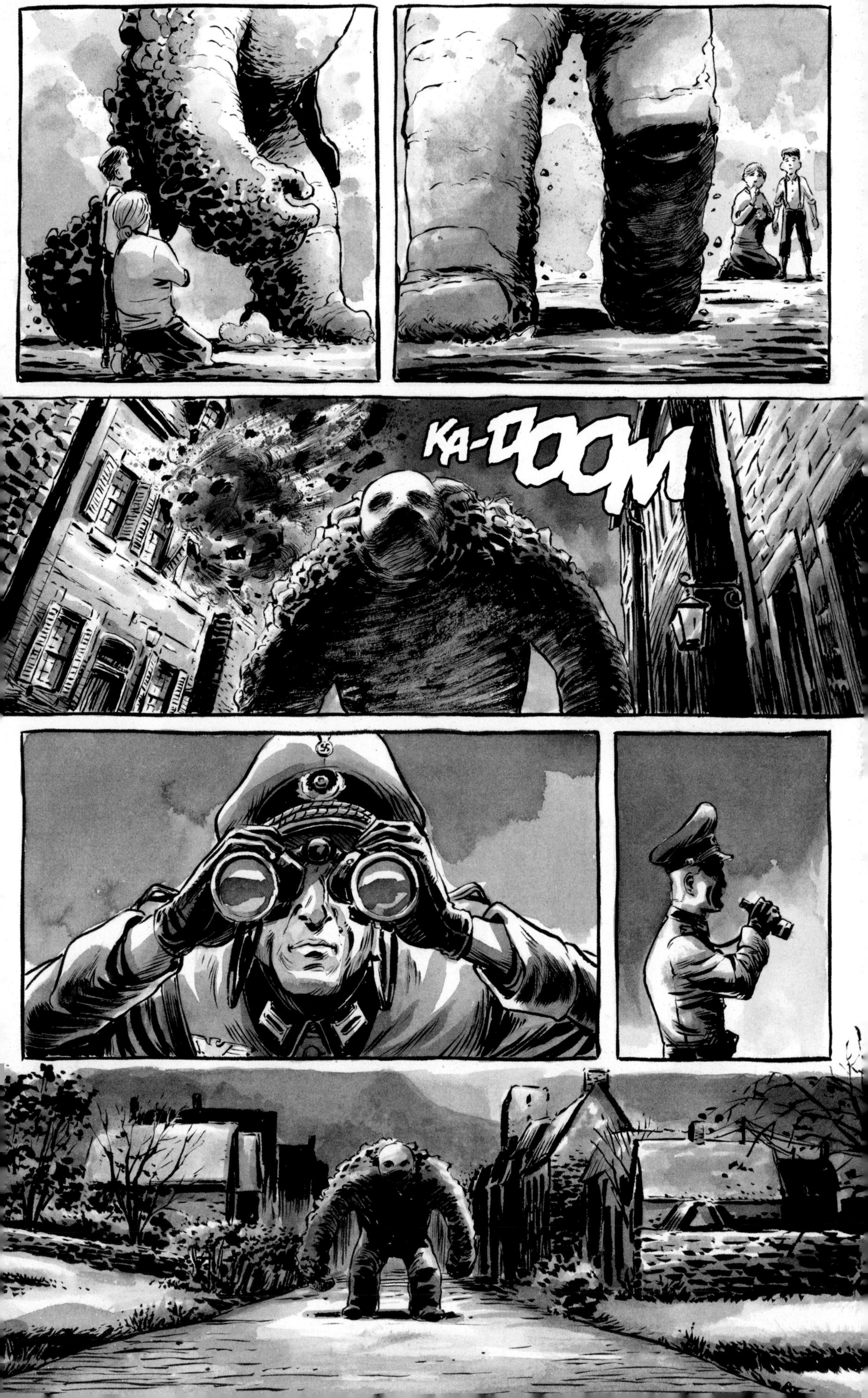
KA-DOOM

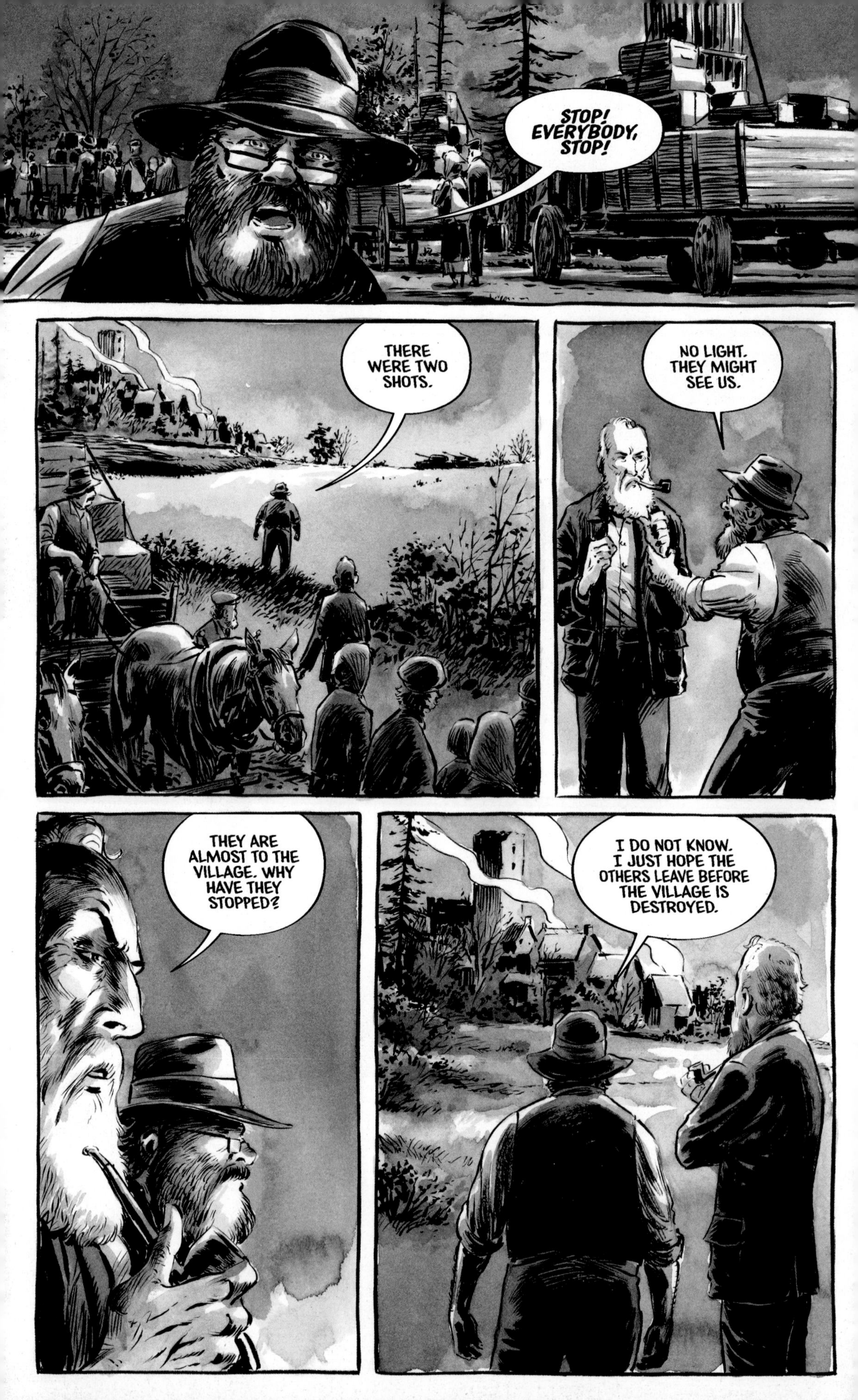
STOP! EVERYBODY, STOP!
THERE WERE TWO SHOTS.
NO LIGHT. THEY MIGHT SEE US.
THEY ARE ALMOST TO THE VILLAGE. WHY HAVE THEY STOPPED?
I DO NOT KNOW. I JUST HOPE THE OTHERS LEAVE BEFORE THE VILLAGE IS DESTROYED.

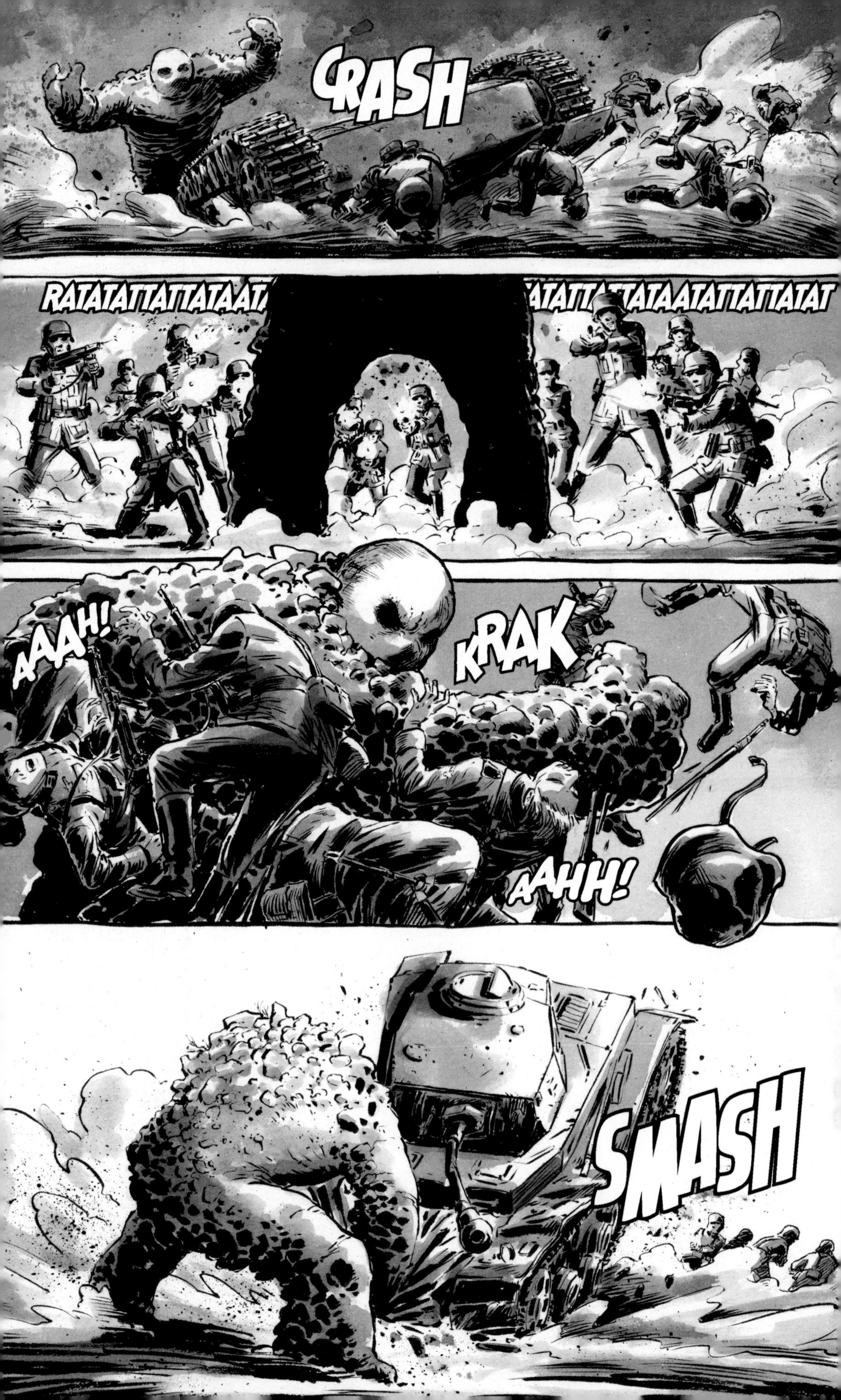
CRASH
RATATATTATTATAATA
ATATTATTATAATATTATTATAT
AAAH!
KRAK
AAHH!
SMASH

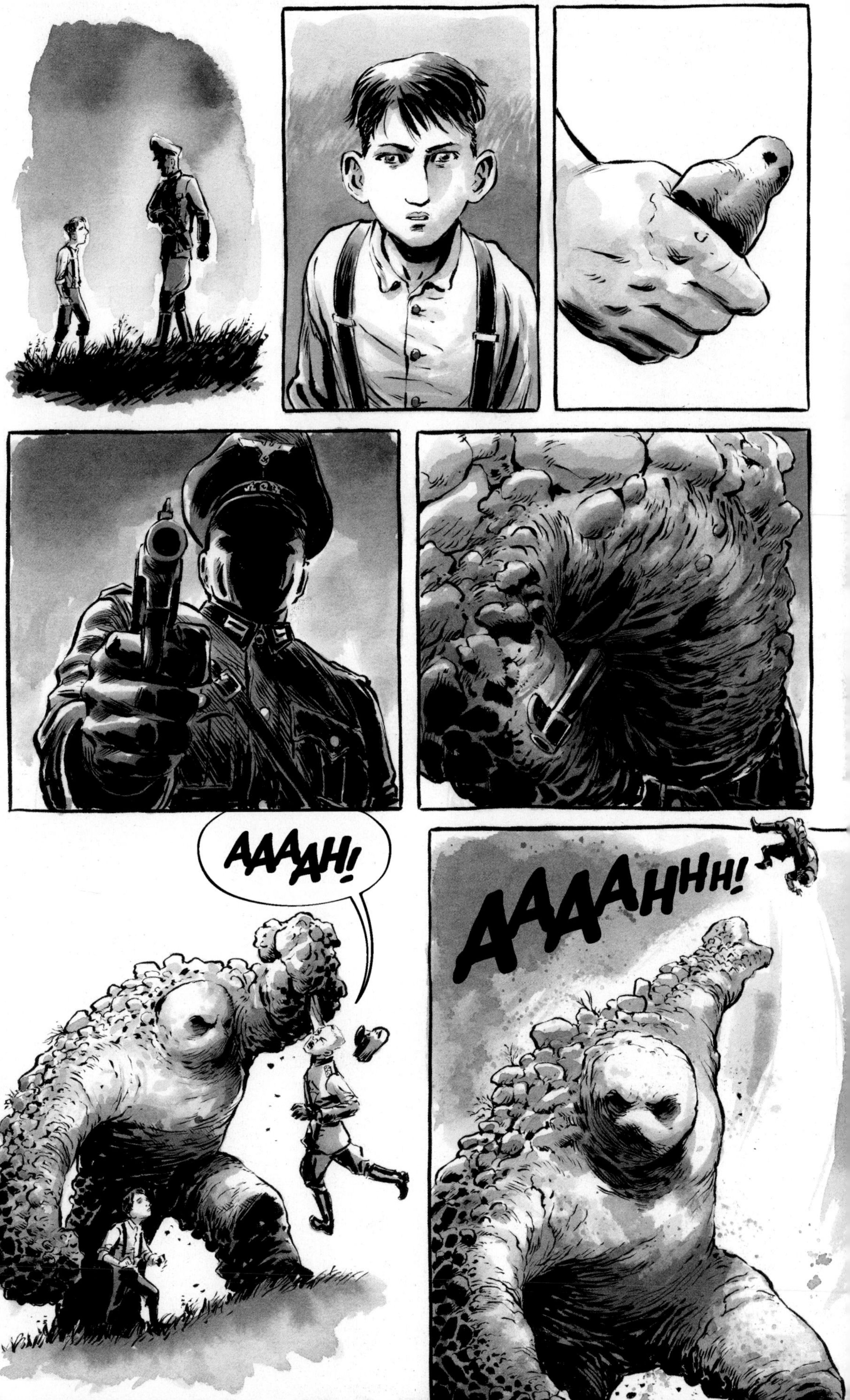
AAAAH!
AAAAHHH!

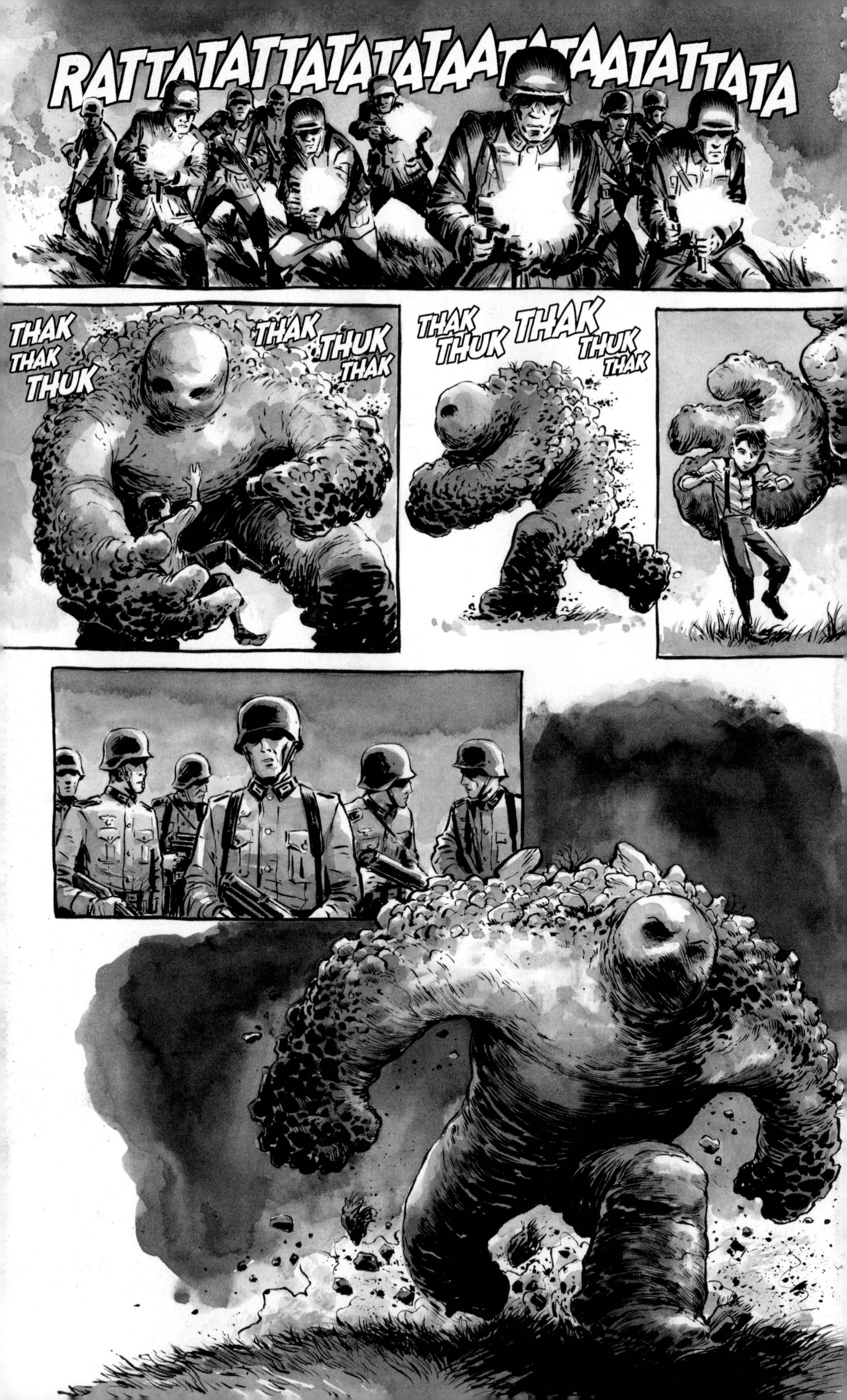
RATTATATTATATATAATATAATATTATA
THAK
THAK
THUK
THAK
THUK
THAK
THAK
THUK
THAK
THUK
THAK

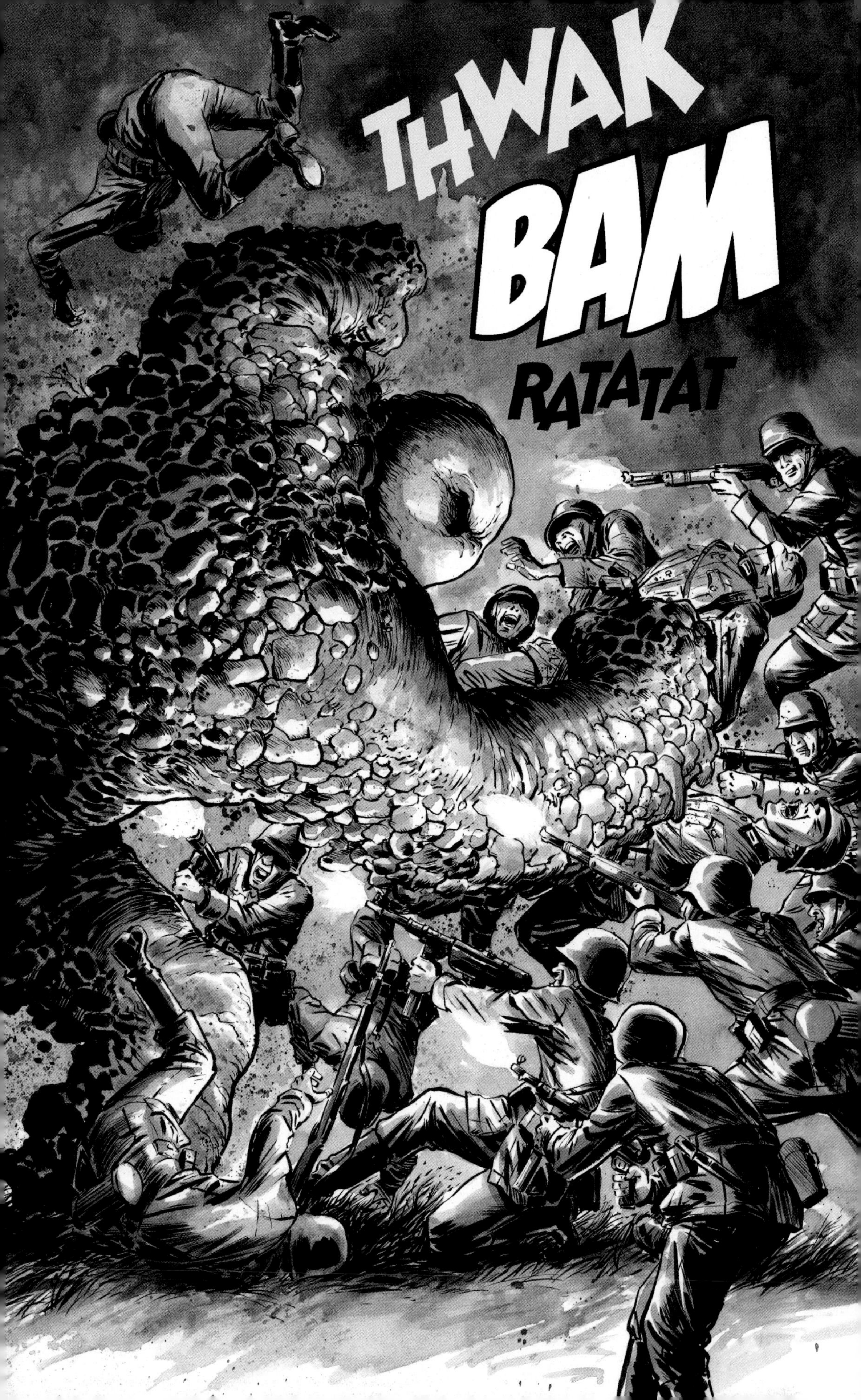
THWAK
BAM
RATATAT

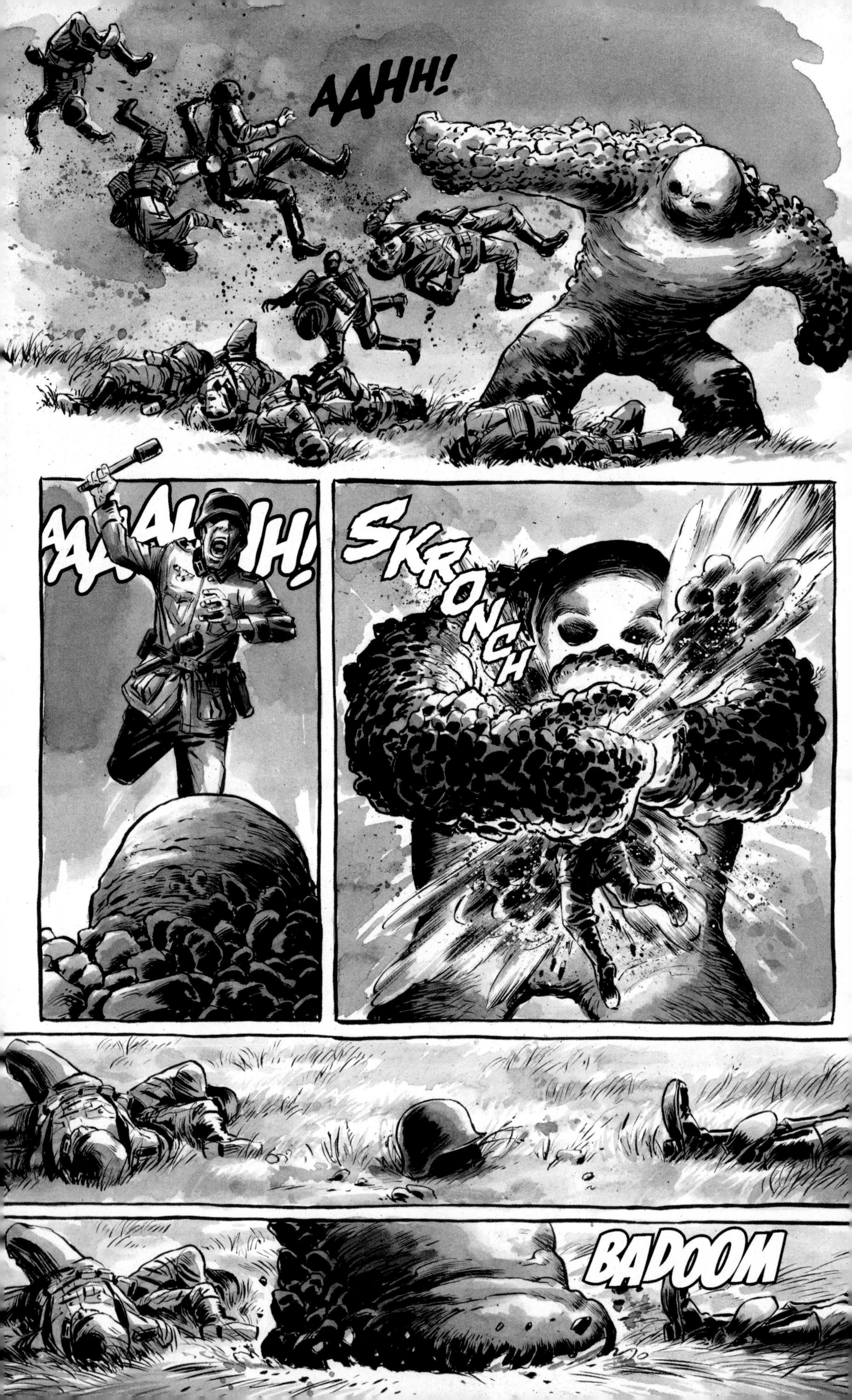
AAHH!
AAAAAAHH!
SKRONCH
BADOOM

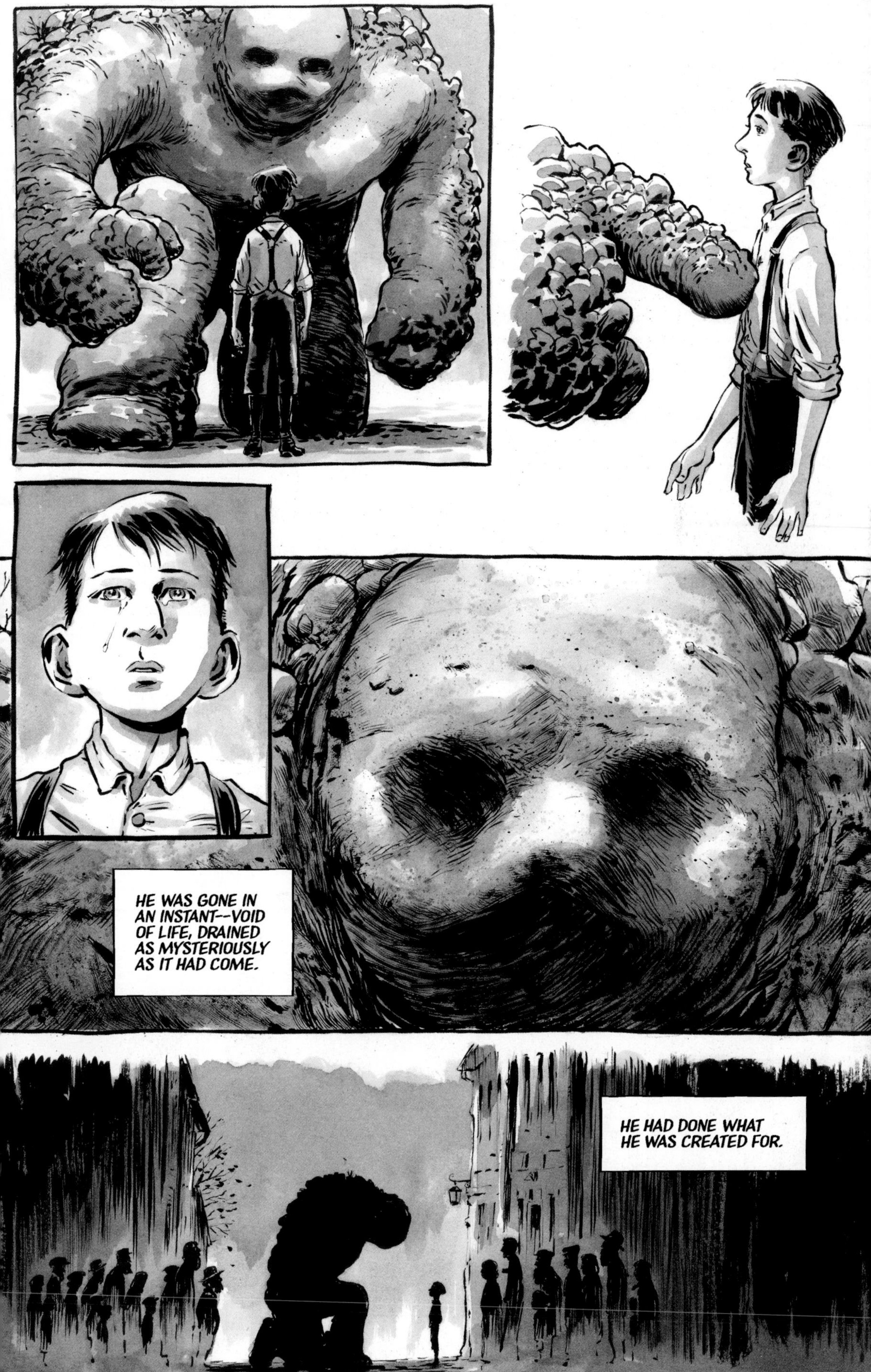
HE WAS GONE IN
AN INSTANT--VOID
OF LIFE, DRAINED
AS MYSTERIOUSLY
AS IT HAD COME.
HE HAD DONE WHAT
HE WAS CREATED FOR.

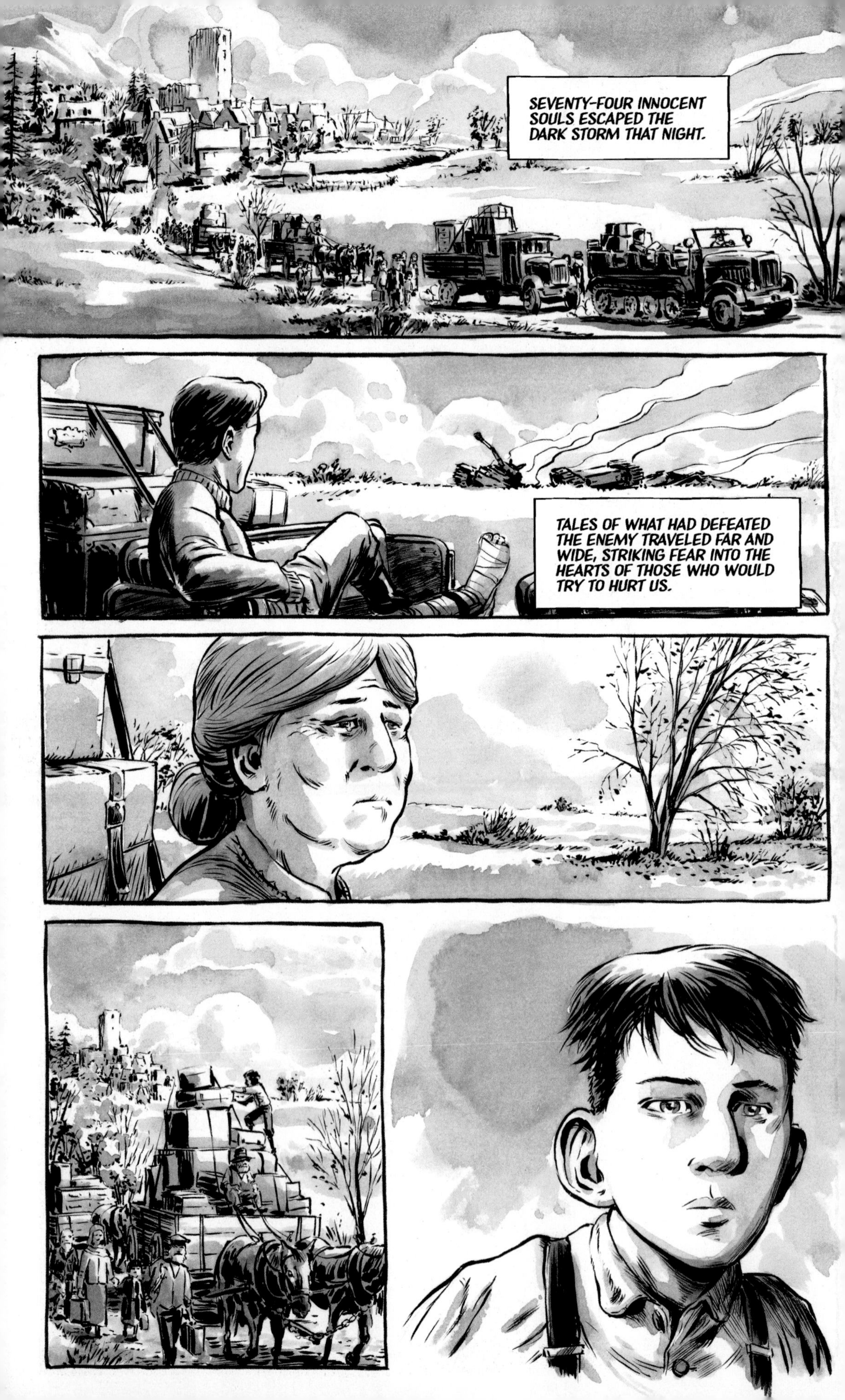
SEVENTY-FOUR INNOCENT SOULS ESCAPED THE DARK STORM THAT NIGHT.
TALES OF WHAT HAD DEFEATED THE ENEMY TRAVELED FAR AND WIDE, STRIKING FEAR INTO THE HEARTS OF THOSE WHO WOULD TRY TO HURT US.

SKETCHBOOK

Notes by Dave Wachter

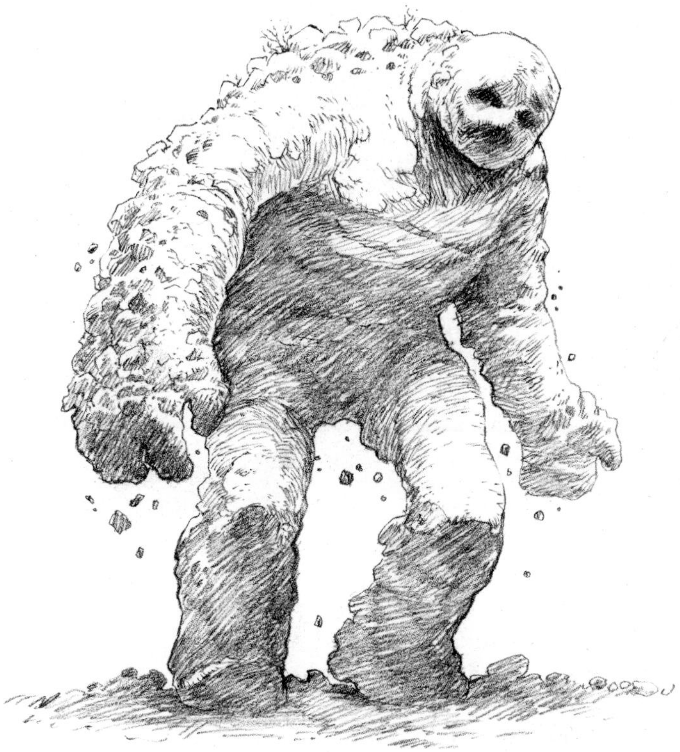

The golem was not crafted by an artisan. It was quickly and haphazardly pieced together by the villagers, with little plan or forethought. Thus, it's a very rough and lopsided design. As the golem stood to life, it dragged clumps of the ground with it. So while its front may be uneven, its back is a muddle of stone and mud, with the occasional plant root. Overall, this leads to bad posture.

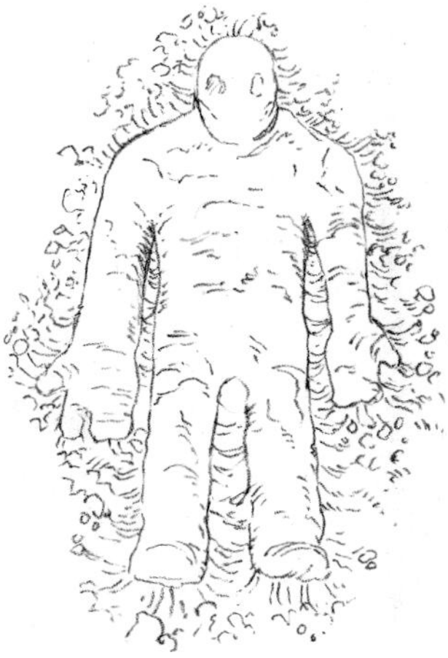

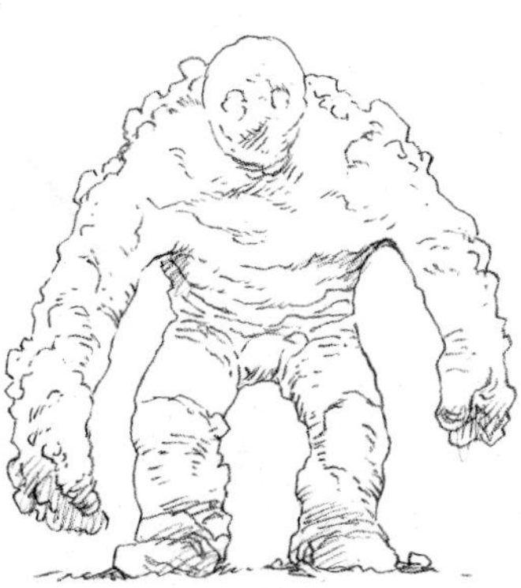

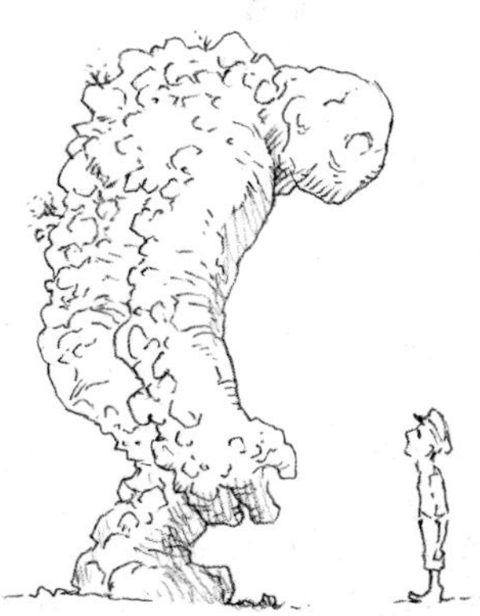

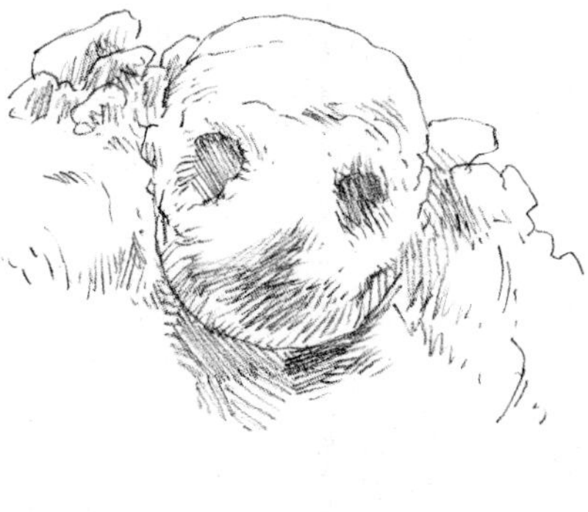

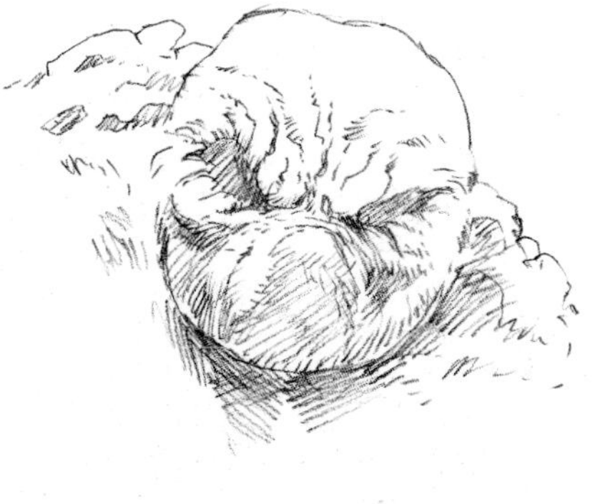

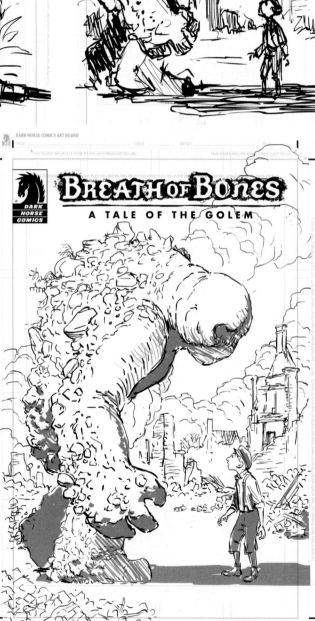

Creating just the right cover design is a tough job for me. After all, I have to sum up the entire story in a single image that will also catch a prospective reader's attention. And often it has to be done without the benefit of the finished script. Above left you see an early design, with Noah holding a machine gun—which, after reading the story, we all can see is clearly out of place. And it's a boring design. There were plenty more where that came from.

The cover for issue #3 (and now the collected edition), right, is my favorite. I love drawing action-packed scenes, but it's the quiet moments that really pluck the ol' heartstrings. This design was originally created as an option for issue #2, but I'm glad we held off for the finale. It's so rare when a work truly encompasses all the ideas I wanted to express. And I didn't mess it up with the watercolors, so I was lucky.

Breath of Bones

A Tale of the Golem

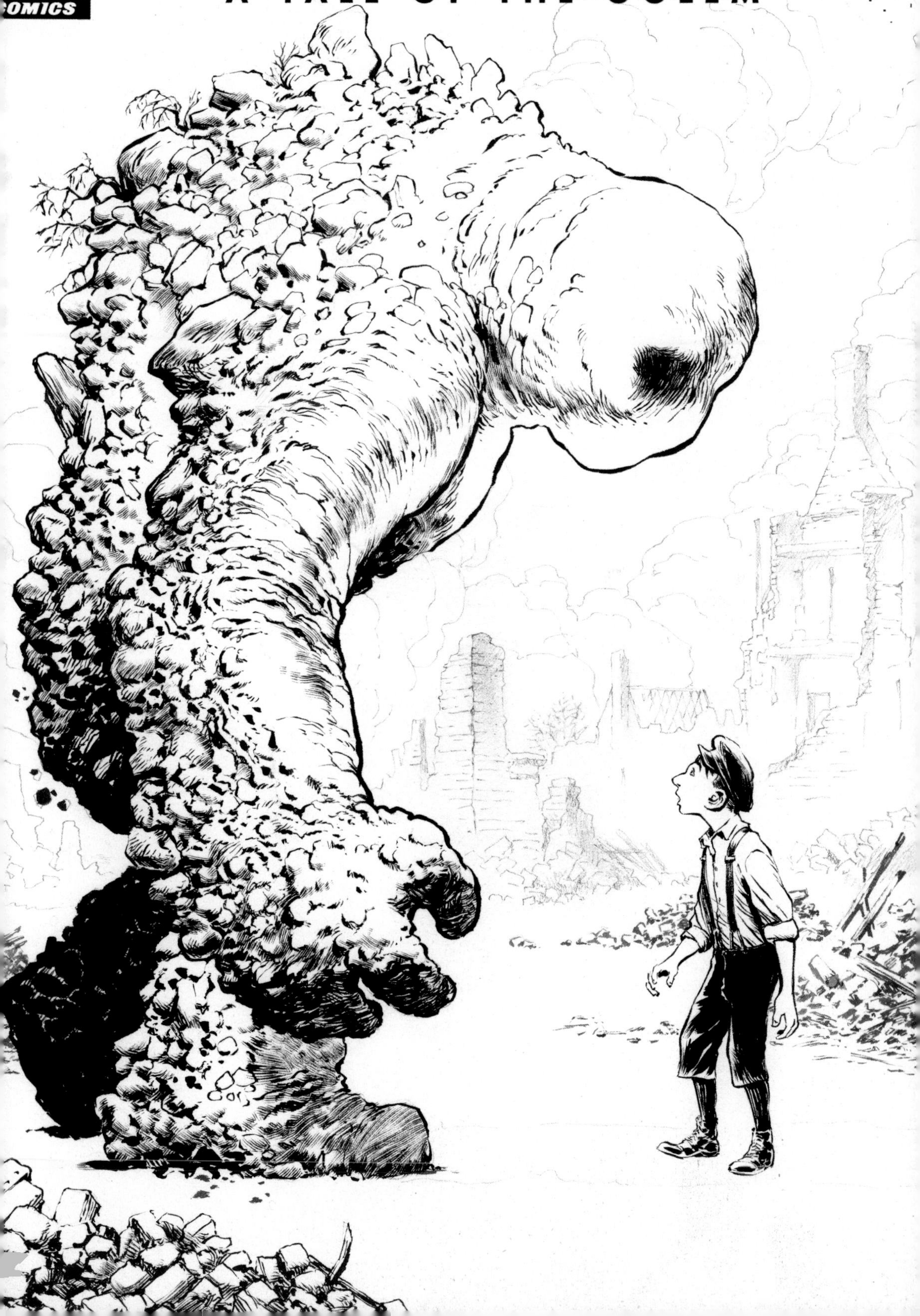

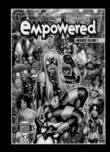